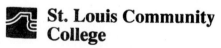

St. Louis Community College

Forest Park
Florissant Valley
Meramec

Instructional Resources
St. Louis, Missouri

GAYLORD

An Oral History of
Abraham Lincoln

JOHN G. NICOLAY'S INTERVIEWS AND ESSAYS

Edited by
MICHAEL BURLINGAME

Sponsored by the Abraham Lincoln Association

SOUTHERN ILLINOIS UNIVERSITY PRESS

Carbondale and Edwardsville

Library of Congress Cataloging-in-Publication Data

Nicolay, John G. (John George), 1832–1901.
An oral history of Abraham Lincoln : John G. Nicolay's interviews
and essays / edited by Michael Burlingame.
p. cm.
Includes bibliographical references and index.
1. Lincoln, Abraham, 1809–1865—Friends and associates—
Interviews. I. Burlingame, Michael, 1941–   . II.Title.
E457.2.N67   1996
973.7′092—dc20   95-36368
ISBN 0-8093-2054-1 (cloth : alk. paper)   CIP

The paper used in this publication meets the minimum requirements of
American National Standard for Information Sciences—Permanence
of Paper for Printed Library Materials, ANSI Z39.48-1984. ♾

CONTENTS

Acknowledgments ix

Editor's Introduction xi

1. THE SPRINGFIELD INTERVIEWS 1

Orville H. Browning 1

John Todd Stuart 7

Ozias M. Hatch 16

Clark M. Smith 17

William Butler 18

Milton Hay 25

Jesse K. Dubois 29

Henry S. Greene 32

Peter Van Bergen 33

Stephen T. Logan 34

John W. Bunn 39

2. THE WASHINGTON INTERVIEWS 41

James K. Moorhead 41

Simon Cameron 42

Norman B. Judd 44

T. Lyle Dickey 48

Hamilton Fish 50

Lafayette Foster 53

Lot M. Morrill 54

William M. Evarts 56

Ward Hill Lamon 57

Leonard Swett 58

Morton S. Wilkinson 59

Stephen A. Hurlbut 62

Lyman Trumbull 65

John Palmer Usher 65

Hannibal Hamlin 67

Joseph Holt 68

Richard M. Hoe 77

John M. Sherman 79

James Speed 80

Godlove Orth 82

Edward D. Neill 83

Henry Wilson 83

3. OTHER INTERVIEWS AND TWO ESSAYS BY NICOLAY 86

Nathaniel P. Banks 86

Dr. Parker 87

Frederick W. Seward 87

A Son of John W. Crisfield 87

Robert Todd Lincoln 88

John G. Nicolay 90

William M. Springer 90

"Lincoln in the Campaign of 1860" 91

"Some Incidents in Lincoln's Journey
from Springfield to Washington" 107

Notes 123

Index 159

ACKNOWLEDGMENTS

I AM EXTREMELY GRATEFUL TO JOHN Y. SIMON, THE GODFATHER of this volume and my previous book, *The Inner World of Abraham Lincoln*. For several years, he has been a constant source of encouragement and support, which is deeply appreciated. I am also grateful to Richard N. Current, Robert W. Johannsen, and Mark E. Neely, Jr., who comprised the jury that bestowed the 1995 Abraham Lincoln Association Prize on this book, and to Frank J. Williams, under whose presidency the Association established the prize.

I am indebted to Wayne C. Temple and Thomas F. Schwartz, who generously read the manuscript and gave me the benefit of their vast knowledge of Lincoln and his times. I also received generous help from Fred Baumann, Katie McDonough, and other members of the staff at the Library of Congress's Manuscript Division; from Jennifer Lee and her colleagues at the John Hay Library at Brown University; and from Cheryl Schnirring and others at the Illinois State Historical Library. Because some of Nicolay's interviews were in a peculiar shorthand, I had to find someone who could translate them. The staff at the Library of Congress's Manuscript Division referred me to William Mohr, who took time from his work on the journals of Montgomery Meigs to accommodate me. To all the above I extend special thanks.

At Connecticut College, Julia Gerl, Tina R. Falck, Regina B. Foster, and Anita L. Allen cheerfully and efficiently typed the interviews for me. The college's R. Francis Johnson Faculty Development Fund helped defray some of my research expenses. Thanks to the kindness of Sue and Edwin Coover, my sister and brother-in-law—who extended hospitality at their suburban Washington home far above and beyond the call of family duty—those expenses were a lot less than most out-of-town scholars incur.

Finally, I would like to thank the lovely and long-suffering Lois Erickson McDonald, who demonstrates Lincolnian forbearance when I am away on extended research safaris and even more forbearance when I am back in Connecticut.

EDITOR'S INTRODUCTION

PRESIDENT LINCOLN'S CHIEF WHITE HOUSE SECRETARY, JOHN G. Nicolay, was born in Bavaria in 1832; five years later with his parents he emigrated to the United States. The peripatetic family at first lit in Cincinnati, then moved to Indiana, then to Missouri, and ultimately to Pike County, Illinois. Evidently Nicolay led a hard life, especially after his father died in 1846. Two years later, according to some sources, Zachariah N. Garbutt, editor of the *Pike County Free Press* in Pittsfield, heard the young Nicolay howling in pain as his mother punished him severely. Garbutt discovered that the woman did not much care for her offspring. The journalist, in effect, adopted the "freckle-faced, red-headed boy in bed-ticking trousers and straw hat" to whom he had taken a liking; Garbutt promised to instruct the lad in the trade of printing. So Nicolay packed a few belongings in a red bandanna and settled in Pittsfield with Garbutt and his wife, who "brought him up as tenderly as they could have done had the child been their own."[1]

In a third-person autobiographical sketch, Nicolay recalled that "Schools were very scarce in Illinois, affording him only primary instruction, and that for very limited periods. At seventeen he became printer's apprentice in a country newspaper office, in which during his stay of eight years he educated himself, rising through all the grades of employment to those of proprietor, publisher, and editor."[2] The office of *The Free Press* became a kind of political headquarters where Nicolay got to know some leading public figures of the region, including Ozias M. Hatch of Griggsville.[3]

In Pittsfield Nicolay also befriended Thomas Wesley Shastid, a boy his own age who remembered that he was "always a modest, perhaps even diffident" person. When they walked about the little town together, the "very, very painfully shy" Nicolay would "shun the streets whereon the elite of the village were most likely to be passing."[4] One day, when Abraham Lincoln asked Shastid where he could get a printing job done quickly, the young man took him to the newspaper office and introduced him to Nicolay.[5] This may well have occurred during the 1856 presidential campaign, when, Nicolay recalled, he first met Lincoln.[6] The following year, when Nicolay's friend Ozias M. Hatch became secretary of state for Illinois, he hired the young man as his clerk. In Hatch's Springfield office, a favorite gathering place for leading Republicans, Nicolay often saw Lincoln. As Nicolay reported, "All election records were kept by the Secretary of State, and I, being Mr. Hatch's principal clerk, had frequent occasion to show Mr. Lincoln, who was an assiduous student of election tables, the latest returns or the completed record books."[7] The two men often played chess at the library where the records were stored.[8] In his spare time Nicolay wrote dispatches about Illinois affairs for the *Missouri Democrat* in St. Louis.[9]

Lincoln came to regard the young man highly. In 1858 he recommended Nicolay to Horace Greeley as a correspondent, calling him "entirely trust-worthy."[10] A year later he assigned Nicolay to deliver the carefully prepared scrapbook of his debates with Stephen A. Douglas to an Ohio publisher.[11]

When Lincoln won the presidential nomination in May 1860, Nicolay hoped to write a campaign biography of him and "was greatly disappointed and chagrined" when that task was assigned to an obscure young man with literary ambitions, William Dean Howells. "But," Nicolay recalled, "my compensation soon came. Only a day or two later Mr. Lincoln appointed me as his private secretary, without any solicitation on my part, or, so far as I know, of any one else. . . . "[12] According to one source, Lincoln had told Hatch, "I wish I could find some young man to help me with my correspondence. It is getting so heavy I can't handle it. I can't afford to pay much, but the practice is worth something."[13] Hatch suggested Nicolay, and Lincoln took the advice. Among his first duties was to make copies of Lincoln's autobiography written for John L. Scripps and send them to campaign biographers.[14] After the election, the president-elect kept Nicolay on as secretary.

Not everyone approved of the choice. Herman Kreismann thought it "ridiculous" because Nicolay lacked the necessary polish and savoir-faire: "It wants a man of refinement and culture and thoroughly at home in fine society. He arranges the President's dinners and parties and all that and a great deal depends on that appointment whether our republican [administration] will make itself ridiculous or not. The idea of Nicolay being fit for such a place[!] I have heard men like [Massachusetts Senator Charles] Sumner, [Charles Francis] Adams and others express more solicitude about that place than any other."[15]

At the White House Nicolay became known as "the bulldog in the ante-room" with a disposition "sour and crusty."[16] A New Yorker complained to the president early in his first term: "If the stories I hear about Nicolay . . . are true, you ought to dismiss him. If he is sick, he has a right to be cross and ungentlemanly in his deportment, but not otherwise. People say he is very disagreeable and uncivil. . . . "[17] Alexander K. McClure, who quarreled with Nicolay about the history of Andrew Johnson's nomination as vice president, described Lincoln's principal secretary as "a good mechanical routine clerk" but added that his "removal was earnestly pressed upon Lincoln on more than one occasion because of his want of tact and fitness for his trust. . . . " McClure claimed that "only the proverbial kindness of Lincoln saved him from dismissal."[18]

John Russell Young took exception to McClure's comments about Nicolay. A journalist in Washington and a clerk in the office of the secretary of the Senate during the Civil War, Young recalled that Nicolay had "great powers of application" and "the close, methodical, silent German way about him." The president's secretary was "Scrupulous, polite, calm, obliging, with the gift of hearing other people talk." In the capitol he came and went "like a shadow." With a "soft, sad smile that seemed to come only from the eyes," Nicolay was "prompt as lightning to take a hint or an idea" and "one upon whom a suggestion was never lost, and if it meant a personal service, sure of the prompt, spontaneous return." Young thought Nicolay a "man without excitements or emotions, never saying anything worth quoting, and in that regard invaluable as a private secretary; absorbed in the President, and seeing that the Executive business was well done."[19]

After the war Nicolay served as Consul in Paris and as marshal of the United States Supreme Court. Most of his time and energy from 1872 to 1890 were spent on the monumental ten-volume biography of Lincoln that he wrote in cooperation with John Hay, who had been Nicolay's friend in Pittsfield and his assistant secretary in the White House.

While laying plans for their book, *Abraham Lincoln: A History*,[20] Nicolay and Hay intended to speak with Lincoln's friends, much as William H. Herndon had done in the years immediately after the assassination. Throughout the 1870s and into the 1880s, Nicolay interviewed dozens of men who had known Lincoln.

Some of the interviews took place in Springfield. "[Norman B.] Judd ought to be thoroughly interviewed, and all the Springfield luminaries," Hay told Nicolay in 1872.[21] In keeping with this suggestion, Nicolay visited the Illinois capital in June and July 1875 and talked with Orville H. Browning, Milton Hay, William Butler, Stephen T. Logan, John Todd Stuart, Peter Van Bergen, Ozias M. Hatch, Clark M. Smith, Henry S. Greene, and Jesse K. Dubois. He returned briefly four years later and spoke with John W. Bunn and once again with Hatch.

Browning's diary indicates that Nicolay took extensive notes while interviewing.[22] In all likelihood these were in Nicolay's unique shorthand, for some of the interviews survive only in shorthand form. In November 1875 Nicolay sent those notes to Hay, with the promise to transcribe them himself.[23] Most of the transcripts, but not the original notes, were deposited in the John Hay Papers at Brown University in 1958.

Nicolay also conducted extensive interviews in Washington. In 1872, with the help of Robert Todd Lincoln he became marshal of the United States Supreme Court, a post he held for fifteen years.[24] During that time he spoke with members of Lincoln's cabinet (Simon Cameron, John P. Usher, James Speed), his vice president in the first term (Hannibal Hamlin), senators and representatives of the Civil War era (Henry Wilson, John Sherman, Lyman Trumbull, Lot M. Morrill, Morton S. Wilkinson, James K. Moorhead, Godlove Orth, Lafayette Foster), generals (Nathaniel P. Banks, Stephen A. Hurlbut, Joseph Holt), and close friends from Illinois (Leonard Swett, Ward Hill Lamon, Norman B. Judd, T. Lyle Dickey). The interviews held in the capital deal mainly with Lincoln's presidency. Some fragments of them appeared in Helen Nicolay's volume, *Personal Traits of Abraham Lincoln*, but the bulk of them have been in the Library of Congress since 1949, seldom used by historians.[25]

Nicolay explained to Robert Todd Lincoln his interviewing strategy in Washington: "There are in this city every winter during sessions of Congress from one to two hundred individuals from whom accessory or relative information on individual points or incidents may be obtained. Many of these are growing old, and in the course of nature will not re-appear here many winters." Nicolay cited the names of several Civil War senators and members of Lincoln's cabinet and declared that "Whenever I can begin the study of special points, I can go to these men for special papers or reminiscences: but it is of not the least earthly use to go to them, until I have a definite inquiry to present. To ask them for general information, would be simply asking them to write a book."[26]

Nicolay in fact did speak with many men about Lincoln. When it came time to write their massive biography, however, he and Hay made but sparing use of the interviews. Nicolay even refused to disclose their existence when Ida Tarbell approached him in the 1890s. She had been assigned by her editor at *McClure's Magazine* to track down people who had known Lincoln. When she explained her mission to Nicolay, he "was emphatic in saying there was nothing of importance to be had," as she later recalled. "The collection of letters and speeches he and Mr. Hay had made was complete; they had told all there was worth telling of Lincoln's life. He would advise me not to touch so hopeless an assign-ment." She ignored his advice. A while later, after she had progressed far, he told her: "You are invading my field. You write a popular Life of Lin-coln and you do just so much to decrease the value of my property."[27] Nicolay similarly chastised William O. Stoddard, who had worked in the White House during the Civil War as an assistant to Lincoln's two prin-cipal secretaries.[28]

Nicolay and Hay were skeptical about human memory. As Hay ex-plained to a friend: "When Nicolay and I came to Washington [to work on Lincoln's biography] we thought we should have great advantage in personal conversation with Lincoln's contemporaries in regard to the im-portant events of his time, but we ascertained after a very short experi-ence that no confidence whatever could be placed in the memories of even the most intelligent and most honorable men when it came to nar-rating their relations with Lincoln."[29] In their preface, Nicolay and Hay stated flatly, "we have seen too often the danger of . . . reliance in the reminiscences of others." More bluntly, Nicolay told a correspondent that most reminiscences about Lincoln were "worthless to history." To Clarence Clough Buel, Hay exclaimed with mock surprise that someone's recollections of Lincoln "had a fair chance of being true, which is strong language to use of a Lincoln reminiscence." In 1885 Hay asked his editor, "Can you remember things? I have to rely exclusively on documents. I would not trust my recollection in the slightest matter of historical interest—yet every newspaper is full of long stories—in the utmost detail—telling us all about the great men and deeds of the past. I, who knew them all, have not a word to say."[30]

Another consideration inhibited their use of the interviews: fear that information reflecting poorly on Lincoln or his wife might be censored by their son, Robert Todd Lincoln.[31] Perhaps the most startling new information in the Springfield interviews, which have escaped the attention of scholars,[32] concerns Lincoln's depression of January 1841. Orville H. Browning revealed abundant new data about Lincoln's courtship, broken engagement, and subsequent attack of melancholy. Nicolay and Hay suppressed these data, explaining that "It is as useless as it would be indelicate to seek to penetrate in detail the incidents and special causes which produced in his mind this darkness as of the valley of the shadow of death. There was probably nothing worth recording in them; we are only concerned with their effect upon a character which was to be hereafter for all time one of the possessions of the nation. It is enough for us to know that a great trouble came upon him, and that he bore it nobly after his kind."[33]

After reading this, Milton Hay chided his nephew John: "I think the explanation of his [Lincoln's] morbidity about his contemplated marriage would have been easier for you but for your regard for Robt Lincoln's feelings. Mr. Lincoln had entered into the engagement in all probability before he had discovered the unstable and capricious temper of the woman he proposed to make his wife. His distrust was of her not of himself. Discovering this whilst hampered with the engagement it became a question of whether to back out or go on, and wrestling with this he became morbid and half crazed."[34] Douglas L. Wilson has corroborated much of Browning's description; other sources have confirmed Wilson's findings.[35]

The Washington interviews, though briefer and more narrowly focused, shed light on many aspects of Lincoln's presidency, including the formation of his cabinet, his relations with Congress, his pardoning of soldiers, and his humor. To supplement these interviews, I have included Nicolay's unpublished essays on Lincoln during the 1860 campaign and on Lincoln's journey from Springfield to Washington in 1861. Each contains fresh information, based partly upon Nicolay's own personal observation. In 1894 Nicolay submitted them to *The Century Magazine*, which chose not to use them.[36]

These interviews must be used carefully, for human memory is, as Nicolay and Hay knew, imperfect. Calvin Coolidge noted wryly that people in his hometown "remember some of the most interesting things that never happened."[37] Similarly, James G. Randall remarked that "The vagueness of reminiscence given after many years is familiar to all careful historical students: if, in the haste of general reading, this matter is disregarded, the essence of the subject is overlooked. Huge tomes could be written to show the doubtfulness of long-delayed memories." Randall acknowledged that historians "must use reminiscence" but counseled that they "do so critically." Even some "close-up evidence is fallible," he noted. When evidence "comes through the mists of many years some of it may be true, but a careful writer will check it with known facts. Contradictory reminiscences leave doubt as to what is to be believed; unsupported memories are in themselves insufficient as proof; statements induced under suggestion, or psychological stimulus . . . call especially for careful appraisal."[38]

But as Douglas L. Wilson has cogently argued, scholars cannot dismiss reminiscences simply because they would not stand up in a court of law: "Observing the evidentiary safeguards of a criminal trial would, after all, bring a substantial portion of historical inquiry to a halt, for much of what we want to know about the past simply cannot be established on these terms." To illustrate his point, Wilson cites Lincoln's youth: "Virtually everything we know about Lincoln as a child and as a young man—his incessant reading and self-education, his storytelling, his honesty, his interest in politics, and so forth—comes exclusively from the recollections of the people who knew him. Non-contemporary, subjective, often unable to be confirmed even by the recollections of others, to say nothing of contemporary documents, this evidence is sheer reminiscence." For all the problems raised by reminiscent material, "the historian or biographer has no alternative but to find a way to work with it and, indeed, with anything that may be indicative of the truth."[39]

Donald Ritchie offers wise counsel for scholars using reminiscent interviews: "Treat oral evidence as cautiously as any other form of evidence. Documents written at the time have an immediacy about them and are not influenced by subsequent events, and yet those documents can be incomplete, in error, or written to mislead." Ritchie notes that a "statement is not necessarily truer if written down at the time than if recalled later in testimony. Whether written or oral, evidence must be convincing and verifiable."[40]

For all his skepticism about reminiscences, John Hay thought anecdotes about public men as important as their correspondence. "Real history is not to be found in books, but in the personal anecdotes and private letters of those who make history," he told a friend a few years before his death. "These reveal the men themselves and the motives that actuated them, and give us also their estimate of those who are associated with them. No one should ever destroy a private letter that contains light on public men or willingly let die an illuminating anecdote disclosing their individuality."[41] This book contains many anecdotes that shed light on Lincoln's character and provide high-grade ore for the historian's smelter.

In order to remain as true to the original text as possible, I have changed virtually none of Nicolay's spelling and punctuation and have resorted to the following editorial conventions only where necessary: Brackets enclose all editorial insertions; words and characters in roman type within brackets represent my reconstruction of mutilated or illegible material in the original; empty brackets indicate the presence of words and characters that could not be reconstructed; and words and characters in *italic* type within brackets were not part of the original manuscript but have been added for the sake of readability. In the rare instances where Nicolay inadvertently repeated a word, I have silently deleted the repetition. Where he left blank spaces, I have used a long dash like this: ———.

An Oral History of
Abraham Lincoln

The Springfield Interviews

CONVERSATION WITH HON. O H BROWNING AT LELAND HOTEL SPRINGFIELD JUNE 17TH 1875[1]

I THINK MR. L'S INSANITY WAS BUT AN EXAGGERATED ATTACK of the fits of despondency or melancholy to which he was subject.[2]

I was here at the time—and when here attending court I used to live in Mr. Butlers family in which Mr. L was then boarding.[3]

Mr. L was engaged to Miss Mary Todd. She was here on a visit living at Mr. Edwards.[4] Her father lived in Lexington Kentucky, and there was some reason why it was unpleasant for her to live at home at her father's.[5] She was a girl of much vivacity in conversation, but was subject to similar spells of mental depression as Mr. L. As we used familiarly to state it she was always "either in the garret or cellar."[6]

She had taken a fancy to Mr. Lincoln and I always thought she did most of the courting until they became engaged.

After an engagement of perhaps a year or so a Miss Matilda Edwards came to spend a winter here.[7] She was a cousin to Ninian Edwards.

Mr. Lincoln became very much attached to her, (Miss Matilda Edwards) and finally fell desperately in love with her, and proposed to her, but she rejected him. Douglas also fell in love with and proposed to her, and she rejected him also.[8]

I think that Mr. Lincoln's aberration of mind resulted entirely from the situation he thus got himself into—he was engaged to Miss Todd, and in love with Miss Edwards, and his conscience troubled him dreadfully for the supposed injustice he had done, and the supposed violation of his word which he had committed.

As I now remember his derange[*ment*] lasted only about a week or such a matter. He was so much affected as to talk incoherently, and to be dilirious to the extent of not knowing what he was doing. In the course of a few days however it all passed off, leaving no trace whatever. I think it was only an intensification of his constitutional melancholy— his greater trials and embarrassments pressed him down to a lower point than at other times.

With this exception he was always a man of very uniform character and temper. He had his moods like other men. He was sometimes jolly and genial, and again at other times absorbed and abstracted—but these alternations were only manifestations of his constitutional temperament—they came and went irregularly. He was sometimes mirthful and sometimes sad, but both moods quickly passed away and left him always the same man.

In this affair of his courtship, he undoubtedly felt that he had made [a mistake] in having engaged himself to Miss Todd. But having done so, he felt himself in honor bound to act in perfect good faith towards her—and that good faith compelled him to fulfil his engagement with her, if she persisted in claiming the fulfillment of his word.

In those times I was at Mr. Edwards' a great deal, and Miss Todd used to sit down with me, and talk to me sometimes till midnight, about this affair of hers with Mr. Lincoln. In these conversations I think it came out, that Mr. Lincoln had perhaps on one occasion told Miss Todd that he loved Matilda Edwards, and no doubt his conscience was greatly worked up by the supposed pain and injury which this avowal had inflicted upon her.[9]

I always doubted whether, had circumstances left him entirely free to act upon his own impulses, he would have voluntarily made proposals of marriage to Miss Todd.[10] There is no doubt of her exceeding anxiety to marry him. She made no concealment that she had very bitter feelings towards her rival Matilda Edwards.

Miss Todd was thoroughly in earnest [in] her endeavors to get Mr. Lincoln, while on the other hand Miss Edwards was something of a coquette. She afterwards married a Mr. Newton Strong who was a young man here with the rest of us in those days.[11]

I always thought then and have thought ever since that in her affair with Mr Lincoln, Mary Todd did most of the courting.

There was never any other occasion to my knowledge, in the whole course of his life which gave the least indication of any aberration of mind.[12]

Nevertheless he always had these spells of melancholy. I have frequently found him in Washington in these very moods. And many times even there, when in these moods, he used to talk to me about his domestic troubles. He has several times told me there that he was constantly under great apprehension lest his wife should do something which would bring him into disgrace.[13]

I recollect one occasion very distinctly when I went to his room in the Executive Mansion and found him in a spell of deep melancholy, such as I have attempted to describe. After talking to me awhile about his sources of domestic sadness, he sent one of the boys to get a volume of Hood's poems.[14] It was brought to him and he read to me several of those sad pathetic pieces—I suppose because they were accurate pictures of his own experiences and feelings. Between his reading and our talking, I gradually got him into a more comfortable frame of mind, and by [the] time I left him, he seemed quite cheerful and happy again.[15]

As for poor Mrs. Lincoln I have for several years past considered her demented.[16]

THE "OWENS" LETTER.

Mrs. Browning has been exceedingly annoyed and chagrined that her name should have appeared in Mr. Lamon's book in connection with that letter.[17] She had steadily refused to have the letter published, until once when Mrs. Lamon was in Quincy making her a visit, when at her personal solicitation Mrs. Browning allowed a copy of it to be made. But even then she only gave it to her upon a promise that her own name should in no wise appear in connection with it.[18]

The letter came into her hands in this way:

In December of the year 1836, when we had been just married, we went to Vandalia to spend the winter. The session of the Legislature of course brought a number of us who had been youngsters together.— Hardin, Douglas, Baker, and myself boarded at the same house.[19]

At that time Lincoln had seen but very little of what might be called

3

society and was very awkward, and very much embarrassed in the presence of ladies. Mrs. Browning very soon discovered his great merits, and treated him with a certain frank cordiality which put Lincoln entirely at his ease. On this account he became very much attached to her. He used to come to our room, and spend his evenings with Mrs. Browning. As I now remember, most of his spare time was occupied in this way.

The Legislature adjourned in March and we went home to Quincy.[20] After we had been at home some weeks, Mrs. Browning one day received at long letter from Mr. Lincoln, giving an account of a love affair of his with a young lady from Kentucky.[21]

The letter was written in a droll and amusing vein, and both Mrs. Browning and myself laughed very heartily over it.[22] We knew that Mr. Lincoln was fond of his jokes, and we supposed that the whole letter was sheer invention from beginning to end.

With that it passed from our minds and we thought nothing more of it, until the time I have spoken of, about the beginning of the war, when I overhauled and destroyed so many of my private letters. When I came across this one, I of course recognized the handwriting. As the writer had now become famous by having been elected President, I handed it to Mrs. Browning who looked over it and said, "We will keep this as an interesting relic of old times.["] Even then she treated it and thought of it as a mere romance and never once thought the letter referred to any real person.

While we were in Washington during the Administration of Mr. Lincoln, a Boston gentleman who had been the publisher, I think, of the "Bobbin boy" came there to Washington for the purpose of gathering material for a similar book about Mr. Lincoln.[23] He came to see Mrs. Browning and said he had understood she had in her possession a very amusing letter written at an early day by Mr. Lincoln, and asked her to let him have it. Mrs. Browning, however, refused to do so.

A few days after this interview she was at the White House, and mentioned the subject to Mr. Lincoln. He then, very much to her surprise told her that there was much more truth in that letter than she supposed, and told her he would rather she would not for the present give it to any one, as there were persons yet living who might be greatly pained by its publication.

On this account Mrs. Browning never did let any one have it until she gave it to Mrs. Lamon as I have told you, and then with the condition that the names should be suppressed.

HIS RELIGIOUS VIEWS

I can't recollect any occasion on which we have ever had any talk about the Christian religion.

He was always naturally a very religious man.

I remember being with him one Sunday afternoon, when we went up into the library (of the White House) together and spent the whole afternoon—I was lying on the sofa on the west side of the library.

I distinctly remember that on that particular afternoon he was reading the bible a good deal—I was reading some other book

Perhaps the nearest approach to any religious talk was in the summer or fall of 1861. We were alone together in his room.

I said to him substantially:

"Mr. Lincoln we can't hope for the blessing of God on the efforts of our armies, until we strike a decisive blow at the institution of slavery. This is the great curse of our land, and we must make an effort to remove it before we can hope to receive the help of the Almighty."

I remember being much impressed by his reply, because it caused me to reflect that perhaps he had thought more deeply upon this subject than I had.

Said he:

"Browning, suppose God is against us in our view on the subject of slavery in this country, and our method of dealing with it?"

I was indeed very much struck by this answer of his, which indicated to me for the first time that he was thinking deeply of what a higher power than man sought to bring about by the great events then transpiring.[24]

THE INAUGURAL.

I was here (at Sp[ringfield]) attending court and Mr. Lincoln came to see me, and asked me if I would not go to Washington with him. I told him that while it was somewhat difficult for me to leave my business yet to oblige him I would make the sacrifice and go.

I was duly furnished with tickets, and did go as far as Indianapolis. But by that time I saw that there was such a crowd of hangers on gathering about him that my presence would only add so much to the difficulties and embarassments which surrounded him.

I told him that I thought it best for him that I should go no further: and after that breakfast at Morton's I returned.[25]

After I told him I was coming back he asked me to go to his room with him. There he got his valise and took from it that printed copy of his Inaugural, and gave it to me, and asked me if I would not read it over, and frankly tell him my opinion of it.

I read it over hastily that morning and told him that so far as I could then see, I most heartily approved every word and line, of it. I said to him I will take it back with me, and read it over more at my leisure, and if I see anything in it that I think ought to be changed, I will write to you from home.

When I got home to Quincy, I read it over again very carefully, and thought there was one little passage which might perhaps be improved. I so wrote him in the letter which you have seen, and I believe the change was made as I suggested.[26]

(Mr. Browning kept a diary or at least some important memoranda about the war.)[27]

I have always regarded him (Mr. L.) as one of the most conscientious men I have ever known.

I have never in our intercourse known him to swerve one hair's breadth from what he considered the strict line of duty.

According to my observation Mr. Lincoln had a tolerably strong vein of superstition in his nature. I think he all his life more or less believed in presentiments. I have no doubt that this feeling had a most powerful influence in prompting him to make efforts for self improvement.

I have no doubt that even in his early days he had a strong conviction that he was born for better things than then seemed likely or even possible.

He was always a most ambitious man.

I think his ambition was to fit himself properly for what he considered some important predestined labor or work.

While I think he was a man of very strong ambition, I think it had its origin in this sentiment, that he was destined for something nobler than he was for the time engaged in.

I have had many conversations which indicated to me that he believed in presentiments.

And I have no doubt that Mr. Lincoln believed that there was a predestined work for him in the world.

CONVERSATION WITH HON. J. T. STUART
JUNE 23 1875.[28]

I FIRST KNEW LINCOLN IN THE BLACK HAWK WAR. I WAS IN THE foot Regt. Thos. Moffett was captain of the Horse Company.[29]

Lincoln was captain of the foot company which went from New Salem. We all went to Beardstown, and from there to Rushville. There the Regiment was organized—our camp being about two miles from Rushville. There they elected me major. I think Lincoln was elected Captain at Beardstown.[30]

We came back home about ten days before the election (August)[31] That was a year of the reorganization of parties. Forquer and some of the other prominent old Clay Whigs had gone over to the Jackson party.[32]

About 15 or 20 of us met in the northeast room of the——and started the Journal.[33]

My present recollection is that it was in the previous campaign of 1831 that Lincoln was elected Captain and I Major of the Volunteers.[34]

In 1832 we went to Rock Island, and from there on to Dixon where we got news of Stillman's defeat. The brigade was then marched on to Stillman's battle ground. From there they marched us to Ottawa, and there the whole force was disbanded.[35]

At Ottawa there was a company formed for 20 days (to serve for an interim until some new reinforcements should be received.) The men were enlisted to serve 20 days.

Elijah Iles became Captain of this new company, and Lincoln and I were both privates in it.[36]

I feel pretty confident that where L. & I went, it was Captain Dawson's company of the Spy battallion—this was in 1832.[37] The battallion was composed of three companies. I think Lincoln and myself were privates in that company.

I think it was when the forces met at Beardstown in 1831 that Lincoln was elected Captain, and that I was made Major on the organization of the Regt at Rushville.[38]

I think we went in this Spy battallion.

On our march we passed where Dement had been whipped the day before—saw the traces of the battle—dead horses &c. We went into Galena after we passed the battle-field[39]

Iles company came back to Ottawa, and there we remained until the new volunteers were organized.

There (our 20 days' e[n]listment having by this time expired) we enlisted (for the 3d time) in another Spy company commanded by Capt Early. This enlistment was also for 20 days.[40]

From there we went with the new army (which had by this time arrived) to a place called the Four Lakes (now Madison Wis.) There we expected to meet the Indians, but when we got there we heard no news of them. By this time our 20 days had again run out and we came home.[41]

I fell in with Lincoln first when he was captain—in 1831 (?) I knew him very well in this expedition. He was then noted mainly for his great strength, and skill in wrestling and athletic sports—in fact he had the reputation of being the best wrestler in the army—he could generally throw down anybody he came across. He was also noted for being a kind genial and companionable man, a great lover of jokes and teller of stories. Everybody liked him—he told good anecdotes and was always very entertaining and amusing—he became very popular in the army.

We had a first rate time on this campaign—we were well provided—the whole thing was a sort of frolic—Lincoln had no military qualities whatever except that he was a good clever fellow and kept the esteem and respect of his men. He made a very good Captain. He had the wildest company in the world—it was mainly composed of the Clary Grove boys.[42]

(RECAPITULATION)

1832. Stuart & Lincoln went as privates in Capt Dawson's company of the Spy batallion commanded by Gen. J. D Henry.[43] Iles was also in the same company. Iles was captain of the mess—I can still distinctly see him cutting the slices of pork.

Route.—Beardstown, Rushville Rock Island up Rock River to Dixon. At Dixon we heard of the battle with the Indians by the volunteers under Stillman. The whole army was then marched to that battle ground; but it being found that the Indians had left, and the time of the men being about expired, the Governor called for new Volunteers to assemble in 20 days.

Meanwhile to protect the frontier during this interim between the disbanding of the old and the assembling of the new forces, the Spy company was organized (at Ottawa) with Elijah Iles for our captain—L & I both being privates.

During this 20 days we marched to Galena—in fact it was a sort of scout to find out where the Indians were. J. D. Henry was with us—and practically had charge of the company. Henry was a military man. There were Indians all about us, constantly watching our movements, and if Henry had not been with us, to take care of us and keep us constantly on the watch we would doubtless have been attacked.

At the end of this 20 days (our time being out,) (and we having meanwhile returned to Ottawa) another new (Spy) company was organized with Early as captain—Lincoln, Stuart, & Iles all being privates in it.

With this company we went to the Four Lakes (Madison) and from there we came home.

Lincoln Stuart, —— & Dr Harrison came home together. Lincoln & —— had lost their horses—so we traveled together "rode & tied."[44]

We got home about ten days before the election. Harrison took about —— and went down the river. I had a horse—we had traveled together—"rode & tied."

We came back partly over the route we went on—down Rock River to Dixon and across from Dixon to Peoria.

We got into the county (Sangamon) about ten days before election—we had a very exciting contest—I was elected and L. was defeated.

In that canvass they attacked me very fiercely—the principal fight was made on me. I have told you that it was during this year that the party was reorganized—that McConnell Cavarly—Green Forquer, May, Ford Cartwright and others who had been old Clay men, had gone over to the Democrats[45]—in fact they had asked me to go with them; and because I refused to do it they attacked me very bitterly—they looked on me as having views for Congress in this Dist., and also as having a chance to win and therefore they were bent on defeating me. I used to be out making speeches and electioneering all day—and came home almost every night to issue a new handbill against some new charge or attack on me. I was bold and aggressive and pitched into them on the stump and charged them with "combination" and "trade" &c.

Lincoln was new then—very few people knew him—he made very sensible and interesting speeches, and although he was beaten he made a very respectable race.

Taylor, Morris & Cartwright were elected as Jackson men[46]—I was elected as a Clay man. Lincoln ran as a Clay man. But he was not then known outside of the New Salem precinct. Sangamon county was at that time very large—it embraced all of Menard and parts of Logan and Christian. It was an immense territory to travel over, and it was utterly impossible to get over every part of it in a ten days' campaign

Lincoln in this race, although he was defeated, acquired a reputation for candor and honesty, as well as for ability in speech-making. He made friends everywhere he went—he ran on the square—and thereby acquired the respect and confidence of everybody.

In this election Lincoln got, I believe nearly every vote in his own precinct of New Salem.[47] This was mainly due to his personal popularity—though not entirely so—for remember this was a bitter fight between the Jackson and Clay men, and there were a great many Jackson men down there.

The complete explanation is found in the fact that the New Salem people were already then interested in a project for getting themselves set apart into a new County (afterwards Menard Co.) and Lincoln being their local candidate they expected to make him instrumental in bringing this about.

This helped to give him the solid vote of New Salem—though mainly it was due to his real personal popularity

(But besides this demonstration of his home strength, he made a very great reputation all over the county.)

Everybody who became acquainted with him in this campaign of 1832, *learned to rely on him* with the most implicit confidence

After this campaign I saw him occasionally—he was then I believe running a store or little grocery or something of the sort down at New Salem.[48]

In 1834 we were candidates again for the Legislature. This time he was better known. All the prominent Clay men here and in other parts of the county were for him. He ran this time by general consent and wish.

Of course there was a strong fight on me again as the Jackson men supposed I was figuring for Congress

I remember we were out at Danleys on Clear Lake.[49] They had a shooting match there. The country people met to shoot for a beef (the candidates as was the custom were expected to pay for the beefs) and we were there electioneering.

Lincoln came to me and told me that the Jackson men had been to him and proposed to him that they would drop two of their men and take him up and vote for him for the purpose of beating me. Lincoln acted fairly and honorably about it by coming and submitting the proposition to me.[50]

From my experience in the former race in 1832 I had great confidence in my strength—perhaps too much as I was a young man—but I told L. to go and tell them he would take their votes—that I would risk it—and I believe he did so.

I and my friends knowing their tactics, then concentrated our fight against one of their men—it was Quinton—and in this way we beat Quinton and elected Lincoln and myself.[51]

CONVERSATION WITH HON. J. T. STUART
SP[RINGFIELD] JUNE 24TH 1875[52]

THE INTERNAL IMPROVEMENT MANIA UNDERWENT SEV-eral modifications. Thus from 1830 to 1832 all the talk was about macadamized roads. The State was to be filled up with fine macadamized highways.

By the years 1832 to 1834 this was all changed. It was then that the Railroad excitement began. There was to be nothing but railroads. Railroad meetings were held everywhere, and the State was to become a gridiron at once.

It was I think in the year 1832 that the first railroad bill was introduced into the Illinois legislature. A Mr. G. Hubbard introduced a bill to charter a railroad over the route where the canal now is[53]

Breese about that time had a magnificent project for a sort of Central R. R.[54] It was to be built by pledging the credit of the State, and was to run from the junction of the Canal with the Illinois River (Peru) to the mouth of the Ohio. (Cairo) Breese finally got his project into the Legislature.

Lincoln and I were then rooming together in one of the up stairs rooms of one of those large frame houses in Vandalia. Breese and ——— had a room just opposite. We had a conference and finally helped Breese through with his bill.

The Canal bill was also under consideration at the same session, and the question was whether the Canal Commissioners should be appointed by the Governor or elected by the Legislature. Lincoln and I made a trade with Breese to the effect that we would help pass his railroad bill if he would help us secure the appointment of the Canal Comrs. by the Governor. Breese's RR. bill came up one morning and was defeated. Then we made this arrangement with him and went back after dinner, got the question reconsidered and passed his bill. In that way we secured the appointment of the three RR Comrs. by the Governor.[55]

(Mr. Stuart must have done the trading.—N.)

There were but few houses in Vandalia then. There were not many members of the Legislature altogether. It was a small body—hardly as many men as are gathered about the Circuit Court here now.[56]

The members were very much thrown together and learned to know each other very well. We had a very pleasant time.

The whole country was entirely new and there were but few accommodations to be had. I remember that one of the objections that were urged against keeping the seat of government at Vandalia was that they did not feed us on anything but prairie chickens and venison.[57] A piece of fat pork was a luxury in those days—we had such a longing for something civilized.

We met each other very often and had a very pleasant time. At first there was very little of party spirit; things were done and measures were carried very much by personal influence and personal arrangement.

The Democratic or Jackson party as it then was, was not really organized until Peck went down there.[58] He was fresh from Canada and we used to call him Canada Peck—he wore a fur cap with a long tail hanging down behind.

He went down there and organized caucuses, and urged the party in all parts of the State to hold conventions.

In all this he was doing a good thing by his party, but the Clay men did not like it, because after he had done all this we found we could not carry our measures as we had done before.

As an evidence of this want of organization in the Democratic party, the Clay men elected all or nearly all the Circuit Judges when the Court bill was passed. The Judges were elected by the Legislature.

Logan, Harlan, Pierson, Ford—the latter was not yet then a declared democrat—he went over afterwards.[59]

Douglas was elected States Attorney over Hardin in order to get the vote to pass the Bank Bill.[60]

It was effected through the man named Wyatt, who expected to be appointed to one of the land offices at Springfield

Somebody else received the appointment however, which of course made Wyatt very angry—so much so that when I ran for Congress Wyatt went for me because Douglas had cheated him in reference to that appointment.[61]

ABOUT L.'S RETURN TO SPRINGFIELD

I was at Washington and with Mr. Lincoln not more than about a week before he died. I asked him the direct question, whether he ever intended to return to Springfield to live after his time as President was out. I told him that I had a reason for asking him the question, which it was not necessary to explain then—that I wished to know whether he intended to go back to Springfield to make his home for the rest of his life?

Lincoln said in reply: "Mary does not expect ever to go back there, and dont want to go—but I do—I expect to go back and make my home in Springfield for the rest of my life."

My reason for asking him this question was, that I thought if I found that he really intended to go back there, I would get a lot of our friends there in Illinois to join together and buy Governor Mattesons's house which was then standing idle, and present it to him—and I had already corresponded with some of the friends at home on that subject.[62]

THE WAR AND PROVIDENCE.

I was with Mr. Lincoln one afternoon and we talked about a great many things It had got to be late—perhaps ten or eleven oclock at night. I finally said to him:

"Lincoln I have suffered a great deal about this war of course—my friends and relatives are all in the southern States &c. I dont think you or any other man can make it go on just as you may wish—*I believe that Providence is carrying on this thing.*"

Said he with great emphasis in reply:

"Stuart that is just my opinion."

Considering our manner of approaching the subject—the lateness of the hour—the emphasis and evident sincerity of his answer,

I think he meant and felt all he said—I am sure he had no possible motive for saying what he did unless it came from a deep and settled conviction

THE OREGON GOVERNORSHIP.

When Mr. Fillmore became President,[63] a number of his friends here who felt that Mr. Lincoln was entitled to some recognition at the hands of the Administration, signed and sent to Washington a request to the President to appoint him Commissioner of the General Land Office. Mr. Butterfield had however got an inkling of what was going on, and made haste to get the appointment through the influence of Mr. Webster, as it was thought at the time.[64]

The Administration however did not entirely forget the matter, and evidently thinking that the paper which had been sent forward was one which ought not to be neglected, determined to appoint him Governor of the Territory of Oregon.

We were at Bloomington (Tremont ?) attending Court together, when a special messenger came up there who had been sent from here with the information that this appointment had been tendered him. On our way down from Bloomington he talked the matter over with me, and asked my opinion about it. I told him I thought it was a good thing: that he could go out there and in all likelihood come back from there as a Senator when the State was admitted.

Mr. Lincoln finally made up his mind that he would accept the place if Mary would consent to go.

But Mary would not consent to go out there.

Speed told me that Lincoln wrote to him that if he would go along, he would give him any appointment out there which he might be able to control.[65] Lincoln evidently thought that if Speed and Speed's wife were to go along, it would be an inducement for Mary to change her mind and consent to go.

But Speed thought he could not go, and so the matter didn't come to anything.[66]

Mary had a very violent temper, but she had more intellectual power than she has generally be[en] given credit for.[67]

CONVERSATION WITH HON. O. M. HATCH, SPRINGFIELD, JUNE 1875.[68]

HON. O. M. HATCH WHO WENT WITH MR. LINCOLN AND OTHERS on a visit to McClellan's Army after the battle of Antietam says:

McClellan showed him (Hatch) at least four different letters from officers in the rebel army, proposing that he (McClellan) should assume military control of the Northern States—that is make himself dictator, and compromise the difficulties with the South.

Hatch advised McClellan to show the letters at once to Mr. Lincoln which he did.[69]

Hatch had become acquainted with McClellan while he was Vice President of the Ill. Central R. R.[70]

One morning during their stay of two or three days Mr. Lincoln took Hatch for a little walk. Reaching an eminence which overlooked the camps, Mr. L. waved his long arms and hands towards them and said to him:

Hatch, what do you suppose all these people are?

"Why," replied Hatch, "I suppose it to be a part of the grand army."

"No" responded the President "you are mistaken."

"What are they then?" asked Hatch.

The President paused a moment and then added in a tone of patient but melancholy sarcasm, "*that is General McClellan's body guard.*"

Hatch also spoke of Hill Lamon's familiarities with the President.

Mr. Lincoln went up there to satisfy himself personally without the intervention of anybody, of the purposes intentions and fidelity of McClellan, his officers, and the army.

CONVERSATION WITH HON. O M HATCH SPRINGFIELD SEPT 1, 1879[71]

THE MACALLISTER & STEBBINS BONDS HAD BEEN ORIGI-nally hypothecated by the State of Illinois for a small sum with privilege of redemption; which the holders, undertaking to force payment at par, refused to allow. Thereupon the Legislature had repeatedly repudiated payment at par. It was now under this mentioned constructive order of Gov. Bissell's that the holders, in connivance with a Republican of prominence had induced the New York State Agency to issue new bonds under a general funding act (?) in exchange for them.[72] Mack was at the bottom of the affair.[73] He went to N.Y., procured the issue and came back to Sp[ringfield] and told me. I went at once to Lincoln. Lincoln came immediately up to my office and sat down and heard Mack's story entirely through without saying a word. Then getting up and stretching himself he exclaimed with his emphatic gesture of doubling one of his fists "I'll be —— if that shall be done."

I was sent to New York and the bonds were taken up and canceled.

Matteson had also helped talk Bissell into the matter.

CONVERSATION WITH C. M. SMITH ESQ.
SP[RINGFIELD] JULY 8TH 1875[74]

IN MAY 1862 I WENT TO NEW YORK—MERCHANDISE AT THAT time had about gone back to old prices—and I went to New York to buy some $40,000 worth of goods for four different stores.

While there I wrote to L. to ask him in substance to "please write to me now and tell me what he thought about the prospects of the war coming to a close,"—not telling him or hinting to him for what purpose I wished the information.

He replied in substance that "he had hoped ere this it would be closed to the satisfaction of all parties; but that now he saw no chance and had no hopes of its being closed, but that it would have to be fought out to the bitter end. You are from the South and know how they feel there about it as well as I do. Let me know how the mercantile community feel &c."

Nearly a year before this—perhaps about the middle of 1861 I had been to Washington—it was at the time Judge Thomas and I brought out the money to Illinois for the use of the troops—we could not send it by express then and had to bring it out in a leather trunk &c.—he took me in his carriage and took me on a long ride, and told me how intensely anxious he had been to arrange the national troubles without war—how deep his sympathies were with both sections of the country—and how hard he had struggled to avoid bloodshed. I was astonished at the intensity of feeling he exhibited, and the evident suffering the great struggle had cost him—We drove down to the Washington Monument—he asked me to guess at the width of the Monument—we got out on the base—and he paced and measured it—then while the carriage waited there we sat down and finished our talk on these matters—

(Smith has in his store an ox yoke he found in the garret of L's house—S. proposes to give it to the State Agl. College in Champaign Co.[75]

(Smith says the model of L's patented boat was also found in the house, and that it has been given to and is preserved at Shurtleff College.)

CONVERSATION WITH HON. WM BUTLER, SPRINGFIELD JUNE 13 1875[76]

I CAME TO SPRINGFIELD IN 1824. THE TOWN WAS LAID OUT IN 1821. It was first called "Van Buren"—I think.[77]

Lincoln first came here in 1829—but he came in [the] manner as represented in Lamon's book[78]

I was in St. Louis in 1824. I took a horse and came up from St. Louis—and went home pretty sick.

Bought place at Island Grove[79]—went back to Nashville and met the boat.

Went away again.

My father died here—left his family—and I was therefore forced to remain here. I hated the country

Went back to the boat Nashville not intending to stay here—remained absent that summer.

When I returned I at once came and made my home at Springfield instead of Island Grove.

I was thus occupied in taking care of my farm and generally looking after my father's family which was thrown upon my care

First time I saw Lincoln was in Henry's store where Lincoln and Johnson and —— Cabanas were hewing out timber to build the boat.[80] Got out the timbers here at the mouth of Spring Creek and floated them down to Sangamon Town about seven miles from where they built the boat.

The boat was then started on the Sangamon river and went down to New Salem and there got fast on the dam.

I was there while the boat was on the dam, but do not know anything about the boring incident[81]

When we first ran Lincoln for the Legislature, he was living at New Salem at Bennet Able's.[82]

Mrs. Able was a cultivated woman—very superior to the common run of women about here.[83] Able, who was from Kentucky, had married her rich, and had got broken down there, and in consequence had come out here

Bowling Green lived about as far from Able's, as from here to Speed's house (1/4 mile) and Lincoln while at work on the boat boarded at Bowling Green's.[84] In this manner he became acquainted with Bennet Able and he invited him to his house. In this way Lincoln became acquainted with Mrs. Able. She evidently liked Lincoln, his genial manner and disposition to make himself agreeable.

By and by Lincoln began to board at Able's. And my opinion is it was from Mrs. Able he first got his ideas of a higher plane of life—that it was she who gave him the notion that he might improve himself by reading &c.

He lived there off and on until he came to Springfield—say from 1829 to the time of the Black Hawk war.[85] He boarded with Mrs. Able—she washed for him and he generally lived there in a sort of home intimacy

Both Lincoln and I went to the Black Hawk war—he as captain of a company—I as a private in Capt Miller's company from Springfield—Lincoln's company having been raised at Salem.[86]

The two companies went from here on the campaign, and we were camped for two weeks at the mouth of Rock River. During this campaign the men followed the usual sports of the camp—they were wrestling, and horse racing. Lincoln being an excellent wrestler threw down most everybody he came to.

We got back from the Black Hawk war about the last of July or August—having gone in April. The following Spring we ran Lincoln for the Legislature[87]

Before the Black Hawk war Lincoln was driving prairie team for Reuben Brown, who was breaking prairie for me on my farm at Island Grove.[88] Peter Cartwright who was then running for Governor against Kinney, came along by the field electioneering[89]

Lincoln at this time was not prepossessing—he was awkward and very shabbily dressed, and Cartwright being already then a presiding elder in the Methodist Church, and dressed as became his station.

Cartwright and Brown agreed in politics—and Cartwright laid down his doctrines in a way which undoubtedly seemed to Lincoln a little too dogmatical. A discussion soon arose between him and Cartwright, and my first special attention was attracted to Lincoln by the way in which he met the great preacher in his arguments, and the extensive acquaintance he showed with the politics of the State—in fact he quite beat him in the argument.[90]

He worked round there all summer driving team for Brown who was breaking prairie in the neighborhood. That was before his Salem expedition (with the boat.)

After our return from the Black Hawk war, in the following Spring we ran Lincoln for the Legislature

(Why did he become the candidate?)

Well it is hard to say just why. It was because of the standing he had got in the county, and especially the prominence given him by his captaincy in the Black Hawk War—because he was a good fellow—because he told good stories, and remembered good jokes—because he was genial, kind, sympathetic, open-hearted—because when he was asked a question and gave an answer it was always characteristic, brief, pointed, à propos, out of the common way and manner, and yet exactly suited to the time place and thing—because of a thousand things which cannot now be remembered or told.

Sangamon county was then entitled to four representatives, and there were about a dozen candidates—my recollection is that Lincoln was run by a sort of common consent without party lines being drawn very tight as to him, but that voters of all parties rather encouraged his candidacy.

My recollection is that the debt for which Van Bergen took Lincoln's horse and compass, was the Lincoln & Berry note for about four hundred dollars. The debt at the bank was about eighty dollars.[91]

The question of bringing the seat of government to Springfield was decided the winter I spent at Vandalia. Duncan and others had bought about 1200 acres of land out here at Illiopolis 16 miles east of here, and had laid out a town there, and were trying to have that made the capital.[92]

I was sent down to Vandalia to work in the interest of Springfield. Van Bergen was also sent down there with me—though he did no good—but to hear him tell it he did it all.

Lincoln and Linder were the two principal men we relied on in the Legislature to make speeches for us.[93] John T. Stuart was the man we depended upon in caucus. Lincoln was not worth a cent in caucus.

You must see Milt. Hay.[94] He used to work in the brick yard in those days, and Lincoln took a great fancy to him. Lincoln and the boys used to go down evenings to the brick yard to see Milt. and the[y] used to roast potatoes and cook chickens there together.

Mr. Butler today (June 16th 1875) showed me an old deed made by Lincoln who was appointed a commissioner under a decree of Circuit Court to convey a tract of land. The following are extracts from the decree recited in the deed:

> Butler
>   vs   Nov. Term. 1839.
> Tilford
>   and others
>   *   *   * It is ordered that Abraham Lincoln be appointed Commissioner to convey the same." * * * "And it is further ordered that Abraham Lincoln be allowed the sum of seven dollars for his services as surveyor in surveying and making report &c."
> * * * "And it appearing that Abraham Lincoln who was appointed to make a survey of the premises in the prayer and ex-

hibits mentioned, has made and filed his report of said survey, which survey is approved by the Court &c."

(Lincoln duly executed the deed on March 9th 1840—the words "March" and "ninth" and signature being in his handwriting—the rest in Noah Matheny's[95]
(Another—a Sheriff's deed to Butler—is in Lincoln's handwriting—a much more rapid and running hand than in his later days.
See also Lincoln's Letters to Butler in my possession.)

CONVERSATIONS WITH HON. WM BUTLER OF SPRINGFIELD, ILL.[96]

M Y FIRST INTIMACY WITH MR. LINCOLN BEGAN IN THIS way:
I have already told you that we went to the Black Hawk war together. After our return Lincoln ran four times for the Legislature—was defeated the first time and then elected three times.[97] I was at Vandalia the last winter he spent there. Lincoln, myself, and two others traveled home together on horseback, after the fashion of those times. We stopped over night down here at Henderson's Point, and all slept on the floor. We were tired, and the rest slept pretty well. But I noticed from the first that Lincoln was uneasy, turning over and thinking, and studying, so much so that he kept me awake.

At last I said to him, "Lincoln what is the matter with you?"

"Well" said he "I will tell you. All the rest of you have something to look forward to, and all are glad to get home, and will have something to do when you get there. But it isn't so with me. I am going home, Butler, without a thing in the world. I have drawn all my pay I got at Vandalia, and have spent it all. I am in debt—I am owing Van Bergen, and he has levied on my horse and my compass, and I have nothing to pay the debt with, and no way to make any money. I dont know what to do."

I had learned to like Lincoln very much. I said to him, why dont you study law? I knew he had got in with Dummer & Stuart, and that they had advised him to study law.[98]

He said "How can I study law when I have nothing to pay my board with?"

I said nothing more to him then. But when we got to Springfield I went and sold his horse without saying anything to him. I went and got his saddlebags and took them down to my house. I had my wife take out what few clothes were in them, and wash them and put them away in a bureau drawer. I also went and paid off his Van Bergen debt, and also a debt he had in the bank.[99]

When he went to get his horse they told him he had been taken down to my house. He came down there and asked where I had put his horse. I told him I had sold him. He was greatly astonished. "What in the world did you do that for?" he asked. "Why you couldn't sell him for Van Bergen had levied on him."

He then went back to get his saddlebags, and they told him they had been taken down to my house. So he came down and asked where they were. I said to him "I have had them brought down here, and have had your clothes taken out and washed. Now I want you to come down here, and board here and make my house your home."

You know he was always careless about his clothes. In all the time he stayed at my house, he never bought a hat or a pair of socks, or a coat. Whenever he needed them, my wife went out and bought them for him, and put them in the drawer where he would find them.

When I told him that he couldn't have his clothes, that they were in the wash, he seemed very much mortified. He said he had to go down home to New Salem. I told him that he might take my horse and ride him down there. I also told him that there were his saddlebags, and that there was a clean shirt in them.

He took the saddlebags and went and got the horse, and rode down to New Salem, and stayed there about a week. Then he came back and put up the horse, and stayed right along at my house for about eight years.[100]

He didn't know for a year or more that I had paid off the Van Bergen and bank debts. Always after that he was trying to do something for me by way of getting even. The first time I was in Washington after his inauguration, the President he said to me: "Butler, now I am in a position to do something for you—what can I do for you?" I said to him "Mr.

Lincoln you cant do anything for me. There is not an office I could fill which would be worth my having; and there is no office it might be worth while to accept, such as perhaps a foreign appointment, which I am qualified to fill. And he never did do anything for me, until he gave me the cotton letter which you have heard about.[101]

CONVERSATION WITH HON. WM BUTLER
SPRINGFIELD JUNE 1875[102]

THE BROADSWORD DUEL.

(THIS ACCOUNT OF MR. BUTLER DIFFERS FROM THE PUBLISHED statements.)[103]

They had a party at Edwards' and Shields squeezed Miss [*Julia Jayne's*] hand.[104] (She was afterwards Mrs. [*Lyman Trumbull*])[105]

Miss [*Jayne*] took her revenge by writing the letters from the "Lost Townships" and probably with Mary Todds connivance sent them to the editor of the Journal by Mr. Lincoln.[106]

The editor seeing the personal nature of the articles, asked Lincoln whom he should give as the author, in case he was called upon to furnish the name. The requirements of gallantry of course left Lincoln no alternative but to tell the editor that he would be personally responsible. With that he went off up to Tazewell county to court.

The publication of the letters of course made Shields furious. He demanded the name of the author, and after some hesitation the editor told him Lincoln wrote them. Shields thereupon being bent on revenge took J. D. Whitesides into his buggy and started with him up to Tazewell county to find the offending Lincoln.[107]

The matter however got noised about and Butler who had been on the look out saw Shields and Whitesides start off. He suspected what was in the wind, and jumping into his own buggy followed them at a short distance, sometimes being in sight but generally keeping so far behind them that they did not suspect his presence. When night came Shields and his friend stopped at a wayside tavern, while Butler hurried on past and in this way reached Tremont before them and apprized Lincoln of what was coming

Anticipating what followed, Butler had also borrowed and taken with him a pair of dueling pistols belonging to ———.

Shields and Whitesides arrived in due time and the published notes were exchanged. When they came to start back to Springfield, Butler went to Lincoln and said to him: "You ride in the buggy with Whitesides, and I will get into the buggy with Shields, and I will propose to Shields that we all stop in the prairie on our way down and 'settle the matter' (i e have the duel then and there.)

Mr. Lincoln did not think this would be the best way to manage it. The parties rode home together as above suggested; but when Butler proposed the matter to Shields, he would not agree to that summary mode of procedure.

At Springfield Lincoln chose broadswords as weapons and Alton as the place. All hands went down there, crossed over to the island, cleared a spot of ground, set up the boards and the duel was about to proceed, when Hardin and English interfered and stopped it.[108]

Butler says he does not know how the matter was arranged—that he had become disgusted with the whole proceeding and was sitting on a log about thirty feet away expecting to see a bloody fight, when much to his astonishment the whole affair came to an end—the seconds suddenly stepping between the combatants and taking their swords from them.

CONVERSATION WITH HON. M. HAY, AT SPRINGFIELD JULY 4TH 1875[109]

IN FORMING OUR IDEAS OF LINCOLN'S GROWTH AND DEVELopment as a lawyer we must remember that in those early times litigation was very simple as compared with that of modern times. Population was sparse, and society scarcely organized, land was plenty, and employment abundant. There was an utter absence of the abstruse questions and complications which beset the law in recent days. There was no need of that close and searching study into principles and precedents which keeps the modern law student buried in his office.

On the contrary, the very character of this simple litigation drew the lawyer into the street, and neighborhood, and into close and active intercourse with all classes of his fellow men. The suits consisted of actions of tort and assumpit,—if a man had an uncollectable debt, the current phrase was "I'll take it out of his hide." This would bring on an action for assault and battery. The free comments of the neighbors on the fracas, or the character of the parties would be productive of slander suits. A man would for his convenience lay down an irascible neighbor's fence and indolently forget to put it up again—and an action of trespass would grow out of it. The suit would lead to a free fight and sometimes furnish the bloody incidents for a murder trial.

Occupied with this class of business—half legal, half political lawyers were never found plodding in their offices. Such an one would have waited long for the recognition of his talents—or a demand for his services.

Out of this characteristic of the times also grew the street discussions I have adverted to. There was scarcely a day or hour when a knot of men might not have been seen near the door of some leading store, or about the steps of the court house eagerly discussion [*discussing*] a current political topic—not as a question of news for news was not then received quickly or frequently as it is now—but rather in the nature of debate and discussion; and the men from the country the pioneers and farmers always gathered eagerly about these groups and listened with an eager interest, and frequently manifested their approval or dissent in strong words, and carried from thence to their neighborhoods, a report of the debaters' wit and skill. It was in these street talks that the rising or aspiring young lawyer found his daily and hourly *forum*. Often of course he had the field entirely to himself, and avoided the dangers and discouragements of an decisive conflict with a trained antagonist.

I found that Lincoln had mastered surveying shortly after I had entered his office.

His mind ran to mathematical exactness about things. Exactness in the statement of things was a peculiarity with him.

He was never a commonplace man. He never went into any company or community that he did not do or say something which marked him as a popular man

The first time I saw Lincoln to know him—perhaps along in '37 or '40 when as a boy I began to notice things—must have been I think in some murder trial—must have been this man (Truett?)—either that or some other that I first saw Lincoln.[110] Of course his rawness, awkwardness and uncultivated manner were most apparent. There was this about it however. I was interested, both because Lincoln was a new man at the bar, and yet also because in the action I refer to Lincoln was expected to make a strong speech in the case, and that expectation was not disappointed.

This old corner over here—Melvins—was a block of buildings in 1839-40 of rather better construction than most others about the square, as shown by the fact that about midway of the block, the County was then renting rooms for use as a Court House.[111] Two of those rooms had been thrown together for a court room. The clerks office was up stairs, and the passage way opened into an adjoining room occupied by Stuart and Lincoln as a law office.

Matheny was deputy clerk under Butler. Jim and I with other boys had been cronies—we were in the habit of running about together as boys do nights and Sundays, and we made the Clerks office a sort of headquarters.

You know that in country towns young lawyers have a way of coming about the public offices, especially those of the Clerks of Courts, into which they are more or less called by business errands. In this way we boys being there together, Lincoln would often drop in on us. I remember the general impression I have that it was always a great treat when Lincoln got amongst us—we would always be sure to have some of those stories of his for which he had already got a reputation. And there was this about his stories—they were not only entertaining in themselves, but they were doubly interesting because they were always illustrative of some good point or hit.

Stuart was away in Congress at that time.

I proposed to Lincoln to go into his office and read law there—he said all right I wanted to read nights; and as he boarded at Butlers, I told him that I would put up a bed in his office, as that would be more convenient for both of us. This suited him exactly, and I did so, and we slept together all the time I was with him. A good part of the time however he was gone traveling around the circuit. I read law with him there, and used to help him in the way of copying his briefs and declarations.

Lincoln as yet was not a recognized leader in politics in that District, though he was one among the recognized Whig leaders in the State. Stuart was in Congress and as yet overshadowed him—he had been longer at the bar and had got a corresponding start in politics

Col. Baker was also very prominent—he was a more brilliant man than Lincoln—but was not recognized as having that steadfast and reliable ability which Lincoln had.

Logan was also a sort of half politician—but his stricter and steadier adherence to the law being a more marked feature of his character.

Hardin at Jacksonville was also one of the promising leaders—and Browning and Williams at Quincy.[112]

At that time all these men rather outranked Lincoln—he was so to speak just emerging above the horizon.

He made a marked advance at the session of the Legislature during which that joint discussion occurred which is noticed in Herndon's (Lamon's) book.[113] It was held here at Springfield

It had become a fashion during every political excitement to have a regularly arranged and organized set-to between the party champions.

On the Democratic side there were Douglas Lamborn and Calhoun[114]

On the Whig side, Logan, Lincoln & ——— [*Baker*]

Each made speeches and replied alternately—the then prevailing issues were discussed to the best of the power of each. The contest was so evenly kept up and the interest created was so great, that when the speakers had all got through, and neither party being signally vanquished, it was determined to continue the discussion.

For this the Whig committee selected Lincoln, and the Democratic committee selected Calhoun.

In this discussion I think Lincoln took a sort of rank, and his ability was received and accepted as an established fact—it was conceded that in a sustained and thorough discussion of political issues Lincoln was in advance of the other leaders.

I remember an incident in this connection:

This custom of public political debate while it was sharp and acrimonious, also engendered a spirit of equality and fairness. Every political meeting was a free fight, open to all comers who had talent and spirit. It was not an exclusive and one-sided affair such as we have in these later times; on all such occasions either side might be represented and heard. The spirit of the times demanded that each party should have a show.

These discussions used more generally to be held in the Court Room, which was in this building right under our office—there being a trap door through the floor which had been made there for some purpose when these were store-rooms. Through this trap door we who were above could hear and know all that was going on in the Court room.

There was a discussion going on—I don't remember whether the one I have mentioned or some other just like it—

I remember that Baker was in it—Baker was always ready for any thing—he was a fiery fellow—and when his impulsiveness was let loose among the rough elements which constituted a large part of his audience, it was generally understood that there might be trouble at any time.

This discussion was going on one night: Lincoln was lying on the bed in office, but the trap door was open and we could without difficulty hear what was going on.

Lamborn was talking, and after a while made some personal charge. We could hear Baker make some sharp reply—then we could hear a sort of muttering—and expected every moment the whole affair would be turned into a general scrimmage.

Lincoln jumped up off the bed, and in about three strides he went down the stairs and into the Court room &c &c.[115]

CONVERSATIONS. WITH HON. J K DUBOIS
SPRINGFIELD JULY 4TH 1875[116]

LINCOLN AND I FIRST MET AT VANDALIA IN 1834, THOUGH there are people in my county (Lawrence) who remember to have seen him when he passed with his father's family through Lawrenceville as they were removing to this State.[117]

Lincoln was at my house on election day in 1840.

There are men in my county who saw him when he drove an ox team through Lawrenceville when they moved to this country. He was then of course dressed very badly—his pantaloons didn't meet the tops of his shoes by a good deal. He was then, generally, a long awkward gawky looking boy.

But when he came to the Legislature in 1834, he was a very decent looking young fellow. He was then dressed in a very respectable looking suit of jeans—it was practically carrying out the protective idea of wearing home manufactures—Henry Clay once went to Congress in a suit of jeans, and it had become a sort of whig dress.

Lincoln didn't take much prominence in the first session of the legislature in 1834. Stuart at that time quite overshadowed him. Stuart had been there the session before—besides he had been practising law, and generally had more experience than Lincoln.

But the next session Lincoln was very prominent. He had by that time become the acknowledged leader of the Whigs in the House. Stuart had gone out and left him a clear field.

Mr. Lincoln was a very creditable member in 1834. But in 1836 he was the leader of the Whigs.

As an illustration of his authority he made Webb and me vote for his scheme to move the seat of government to Springfield.[118] We belonged to the southern end of the State. We defended our vote before our constituents by saying that necessity would ultimately force the seat of government to a central position. But in reality we gave the vote to Lincoln because we liked him and because we wanted to oblige our friend, and because we recognized his authority as our leader.[119]

Douglas was also in the House at that session, but he had nothing like the prominence that Lincoln had.

Mr. Lincoln then went along gradually and came up. Why he didn't in those days control this Congressional District better than he did, I never did know.

Stuart used to be called "Jerry Sly" down there at Vandalia, while up here the "Register" called him "Sleepy John."[120]

Lincoln was always the party here—and the party has been good for nothing here since he has been gone.

Before that first session of 1834 was over, Lincoln was already a prominent man. Our very first impression of him was that he was more than an ordinary man.

The Whig party was very weak then, and those who believed that way worked together

I think I never saw him stumped but once. That was on the passage of the legislation about removing the seat of government. Webb, Wilson, and myself roomed together in 1836.[121] Wilson, Blankenship, Gov. Duncan and John Taylor had entered a great lot of land, and laid out the town of Illiopolis, and were engaged in an effort to get the seat of government moved there.[122] From our being such constant companions, Wilson had every right to suppose that Webb and I were his friends in that measure.

Lincoln came to my room one evening and told me that he was whipped—that his career was ended—that he had traded off everything he could dispose of, and still had not got strength enough to locate the seat of government at Springfield—"and yet" said he "I cant go home without passing that bill. My folks expect that of me, and that I cant do—and I am finished forever."

I said to him "well Lincoln, there is but one thing for you to do."

"Well" said he "tell me how that is to be done."

I said to him "first pass the bill to move the seat of government, and Springfield, Jacksonville, Peoria, and every other town that expects to get the seat of government will vote for that bill, Vandalia alone excepted. Then pass a joint resolution, locating the seat of government, and for beginning a suitable building so as to have it ready by the time provided in the Constitution for moving it."

"By jings" said he "I reckon that will do it." And he had a bill ready that night, and we passed it. When we went into joint session the other fellows saw the trap, but it was too late. We carried the measure for Springfield, and old Wilson wouldn't speak to Webb or me for a week afterward.

Mr. Lincoln was always a good man. There was never anything mean about him. He never played any tricks on anybody.[123]

CONVERSATION WITH HON. H. S. GREENE
SP[RINGFIELD] JULY 1875[124]

DEBATE AT CLINTON

HON. H. S. GREENE SAYS THAT THE CAMPAIGN OF 1858 WAS opened at Clinton.[125] Douglas came there and made his speech attacking Mr. Lincoln fiercely, it being the Little Giant's first reply to the charge of conspiracy which Mr. Lincoln had made against him.[126]

Lincoln and Judge Davis sat on the platform beside Douglas and heard him through. This was in the afternoon. There was a very large crowd in attendance, and Douglas had made one of his powerful and denunciatory attacks. Everybody was very much excited.

When Douglas concluded, Lincoln arose pale and trembling evidently wrought up to the highest pitch. But he simply asked that such of his friends as desired to hear his side of the question would remain and come to the Court House at candle-light, where he would reply to Douglas

Greene and other Republicans then went to work to get up a good crowd. By way of making it more impressive they designated a place in the outskirts of the town where the people should meet and form a procession, and march to the Court House.

When Lincoln went up into the Court house to begin the meeting there were but two or three dozen in the room. Lincoln was very much depressed, still smarting under the fierceness of the assault Douglas had made upon him. He mounted the platform and began his speech, saying there were but very few present—but that as he had made the announcement that he would speak, and as they had probably stayed or come for the express purpose of hearing him, he felt it was due to them that he should fulfil his promise. He would therefore go on and reply to Douglas in full—notwithstanding the smallness of the meeting. He regretted indeed to see so few present, for [it] indicated to him that the people did not take the same interest in the views of himself and his friends, that they did in those of their opponents. &c &c

About this time Greene's procession began to arrive, and soon filled the room to overflowing, and forming in the aggregate quite as large an audience as that which Douglas had addressed in the afternoon.

Upon this inspiration Lincoln began to cheer up and finally warmed himself into a very successful oratorical effort.

CONVERSATION WITH P. VAN BERGEN
SP[RINGFIELD] JULY 7TH 1875[127]

DOES NOT—OR DOES NOT WANT TO—REMEMBER ANYTHING about the levy and sale of Mr. Lincolns compass & horse in the year (?)

Mr. Lincoln was a good surveyor I employed him to go with me and lay out a town on the Mississippi River. Iles had loaned some people some money and they couldn't pay it, and he took on 80 acres of Land—and Iles thought it might be a good thing to lay out a town on it, and said he would give me a share in it if I would attend to having it surveyed &c. There were three of us in partnership.

We traveled over there on horseback—found stopping places on the road—stayed there about a week, and Lincoln surveyed and laid out the town site—he did it all himself, without help from anybody except chainmen &c. and also made a plat of it.

Burlington was I think already laid out then—though it was as yet not much of a place.

Lincoln was understood to be a good surveyor then. We traveled on horseback from here there—there was a man living on the land and a little settlement about there—The place is opposite the mouth of the Iowa river

We started from here when they had the cholera—I had some good brandy with me and used to take it as a preventive of cholera—but Lincoln always refused to take any even for that purpose. People sometimes refused to let us stay all night when they found we were from Sp[ringfield] where the cholera was.

At New Salem L. used to be amongst very rough people—among drinking people, though he never drank himself

Stuart, Logan, Iles & I went down to Vandalia the winter the seat of Govt was changed. I helped a great deal to drum up the members when it came to a vote. We had votes enough to carry out our project, but they were not always on hand—would be off taking a drink &c—I used to go after them to the saloons &c. I spent about $1000 in treating &c.

CONVERSATION WITH HON. S. T. LOGAN AT SPRINGFIELD JULY 6, 1875[128]

I CAME TO SPRINGFIELD ON THE 16TH OF MAY 1832—WAS HERE during part of the excitement which attended the arrival of the "Talisman," though that excitement had by that time received something of a check, as the boat in going out of the river was nearly torn to pieces.[129]

That was a very wet season—all the flat lands south of here were covered with water—I suppose I rode for a mile south of here with the water up to my horse's legs.

Then there came a great change in the weather. After the 16th of May I think there was but one shower until the 7th of September and that just only enough to wet the dust. I dont think I have seen so dry a season here since. That summer it was quite common to see the soil cracked open. I have seen it in places so that I could put my hand down into the crack.

Very soon after I came I began to get the symptoms of the chills and fever, and then I wished I had never left Kentucky. But then I couldn't get away; I would have left if I could have done so. In those days I have often seen ten wagons going back to where I saw one coming this way.

In those days we were bringing seed corn from Kentucky, and all our flour came from Cincinnati. Money was very scarce—I have paid $1 per bushel for corn to feed my horse.

That was the year of the Black Hawk war—the troops came through here, and the road from here to Sangamon river was all dust for one hundred yards wide, where there was low brush. The Sangamon river was so low that year that by laying a few rocks, one could cross it dry shod almost any where.

Many people doubted then whether this country could be inhabited at all. I would have gone right back to Kentucky if I could have had a railroad to go on.

I became acquainted with Lincoln that year. They were making a canvass for the legislature. I had very soon got acquainted with Stuart, because we were both Whigs.

Stuart and Lincoln were the only two men who attracted my attention in that canvass.

I never saw Lincoln until he came up here to make a speech. I saw Lincoln before he went up into the stand to make his speech. He was a very tall and gawky and rough looking fellow then—his pantaloons didn't meet his shoes by six inches. But after he began speaking I became very much interested in him. He made a very sensible speech.

It was the time when Benton[130] was running his theory of a gold circulation. Lincoln was attacking Benton's theory and I thought did it very well.

It was a speech of perhaps half an hour long. All the candidates made speeches. The meeting was held at the old Court House where the present State House stands.

This county was then very large. In addition to Sangamon it embraced all of Logan, Menard, part of Mason, and most of Christian. In addition to the speeches at the Court House they used to have a good many fights at the groceries. Two gangs of country bullies used to meet here and fight one another. One was from Lick Creek, and the other from Spring Creek. I had seen a good deal of that sort of thing in Kentucky, and was somewhat used to it, but a stranger would have considered this a pretty hard country, I suppose. All the candidates made speeches at the meetings in those times, but nobody else.

The manner of Mr. Lincoln's speech then was very much the same as his speeches in after life—that is the same peculiar characteristics were apparent then, though of course in after years he evinced both more knowledge and experience. But he had then the same novelty and the same peculiarity in presenting his ideas. He had the same individuality that he kept up through all his life.

I knew nothing then about his avocation or calling at New Salem. The impression that I had at the time was that he was a sort of loafer down there.

I think that about that time he had concluded to quit work as a common day laborer, and try to make his living in some other way. Up to that time I think he had been doing odd jobs of surveying, and one thing and another.

But one thing we very soon learned was that he was immensely popular, though we found that out more at the next election than then.

In 1832 while he got a very large vote in his own precinct of New Salem, they hadn't voted for him very well in other parts of the county. This made his friends down there very mad, and as they were mostly democratic, but were for Lincoln on personal grounds, in the next race (1834) they told their democratic brethren in the other parts of the county that they must help elect Lincoln, or else they wouldn't support the other democratic candidates. This they did purely out of their personal regard for him, and through that influence he was elected in 1834. That was the general understanding of the matter here at the time. In this he made no concession of principle whatever. He was as stiff as a man could be in his Whig doctrines. They did this for him simply because he was popular—because he was Lincoln.

He showed his superiority among them right away even yet while he was making rails. I believe he worked for a man named Kirkpatrick for awhile.[131]

He was always very independent and had generally a very good nature. Though he had at times, when he was roused, a very high temper. He controlled it then in a general way, though it would break out sometimes—and at those times it didn't take much to make a him whip a man. He wanted to whip Judge Jesse Thomas here once in a canvass for an election.[132] It was after he had been elected a time or two—perhaps in 1840. The court was sitting here at the time, and the crowd was in the Court House listening to the electioneering speeches.

In the election of 1832 he made a very considerable impression upon me as well as upon other people.

In the campaign of 1834 he was much more known though I knew personally less about that canvass than in that of 1832. I was then practicing law and was attending to my work and studies. I was on the bench in 1836—was elected in the spring of 1835, and remained until 1837.

He (L.) was at the head of the project to remove the seat of government here; it was entirely entrusted to him to manage. The members were all elected that session upon one ticket. But they all looked to Lincoln as the head.

I was in Vandalia that winter and had a talk with Lincoln there. I remember that I took him to task for voting for the Internal Improvement scheme. He seemed to acquiesce in the correctness of my views as I presented them to him. But he said he couldn't help himself—he had to vote for it in order to secure the removal here of the seat of government.[133]

My partnership with him in the practice of law was formed in 1841. I had had Baker before that. But I soon found I could not trust him in money matters. He got me into some scrapes by collecting and using money though he made it all right afterwards. You know Baker was a perfectly reckless man in matters of money. Baker was a pretty good lawyer. When he would try he could manage his materials as well as most men.

Lincoln's knowledge of law was very small when I took him in. There were no books out here in those days worth speaking of.

I dont think he studied very much. I think he learned his law more in the study of cases. He would work hard and learn all there was in a case he had in hand. He got to be a pretty good lawyer though his general knowledge of law was never very formidable. But he would study out his case and make about as much of it as anybody. After a while he began to pick up a considerable ambition in the law. He didn't have confidence enough at first.

He had been in partnership with Stuart, and Stuart never went much upon the law. Things have changed very much here since then. Lawyers must know very much more now than they needed to do in those times. Stuart was never a reader of law; he always depended more on the management of his case.

After Lincoln went in with me he turned in to try to know more and studied to learn how to prepare his cases.

I think he began reading perhaps a couple of years before he came up here. He used to come up here and borrow a book at a time and take it down there with him to read

While he was down there at New Salem I think his time was mainly given to fun and social enjoyment and in the amusements of the people he came daily in contact with. After he came here to Springfield however he got rid to a great degree of this disposition. Both he and Baker were exceedingly useful to me in getting the good will of juries. Lincoln seemed to put himself at once on an equality with everybody—never of course while they were outrageous, never while they were drunk or noisy or anything of the kind.

I never in my life saw Lincoln taste liquor. In going around the circuit with him I sometimes myself got and took a little after having got wet in a storm, or swam a creek, or something of the sort; but he didn't even take it then. I never saw him taste liquor in my life, of all the times that we were traveling together.

Our law partnership continued perhaps three years.[134] I then told him that I wished to take in my son David with me who had meanwhile grown up, and Lincoln was perhaps by that time quite willing to begin on his own account. So we talked the matter over and dissolved the partnership amicably and in friendship.

In that time he had made considerable progress. I recollect very well an observation I made to him about that time on an occasion when he had got very much discouraged. He had been over about Danville on the circuit and Baker had got very much the advantage of him in some matters there. He came and complained to me that Baker had got so much the start of him that he despaired of getting even with him in acquirements and skill.

I said to him: "it does not depend on the start a man gets, it depends on how he keeps up his labors and efforts until middle life."

I think he remembered and acted upon that advice, for he spoke to me several times and mentioned the comfort and assistance he had derived from it.

Baker was a brilliant man but very negligent: while Lincoln was growing all the time, from the time I first knew him. He was not much of a reader. Lincoln was never what might be called a very industrious reader. But he would get a case and try to know all there was connected with it; and in that way before he left this country he got to be quite a formidable lawyer.

But he had this one peculiarity: he couldn't fight in a bad case.

So far as his reading and knowledge of law went he had a quite unusual grasp of the principles involved. When he was with me, I have seen him get a case and seem to be bewildered at first, but he would go at it and after a while he would master it. He was very tenacious in his grasp of a thing that he once got hold of.

In 1840 Lincoln was one of the Harrison electors, and took a long trip, making stump speeches down south and over on the Wabash.[135] It seemed to be supposed that his character and style of speaking suited the people down there more than up north

His first trial here of importance was the prosecution against Truett for the murder of Early.[136] Stuart was employed but at the time was away in Congress. In that Lincoln made a short but strong and sensible speech.

Douglas and Woodson,[137] then prosecuting Attorney were on one side and Lincoln, Logan and Baker defending.

CONVERSATION WITH JOHN W BUNN, SPRINGFIELD AUG. 21 1879[138]

IN THE SENATORIAL ELECTION IN 1855, IT WAS GENERALLY UNderstood and believed that the 5 Anti-Nebraska Democrats would vote for Matteson, in case Trumbull were not chosen.[139] Matteson being governor, and reputed wealthy had made himself socially very agreeable to the people of Springfield, and the legislature generally. He was in his paling days. His personal friends had been extremely busy in electioneering. Goodell told me that morning that Matteson would be the next U S Senator.[140] The popular tide was running largely in his favor.

The hall and galleries were packed—there was intense excitement when the solid democratic vote was changed from Shields to Matteson. Then Lincoln urged his friends to vote for Trumbull. They did so with the most obstinate reluctance. It was only after Lincoln had begged him to do so that Logan amid breathless silence got up and changed his vote, and Trumbull was chosen.

Even then the whigs for the most part felt sorry for what had occurred. There was a party that night at Ninian Edwards: Lincoln was the
lion of the evening—surrounded with condoling friends most of whom
told him they would have preferred Matteson to Trumbull. But Lincoln
reassured them and told them it was all right &c.

The Washington Interviews

CONVERSATION WITH HON J. K. MOREHEAD AT WASHINGTON MAY 12TH & 13TH 1880[1]

I ASKED MR. M. WHETHER HE REMEMBERED HIS VISIT TO Springfield in January 1861 at Cameron's instance or in his behalf, or the circumstances or conversation relating to his bringing back with him a letter from Mr. L to C. being simply a line inviting C. to visit him again at Springfield.)

I remember the visit very well. Mr. Alex. Cummings went with me.[2] We went at Cameron's instance to induce Mr. L. to appoint him into the Cabinet. We had letters of introduction. When we arrived at Springfield we met Judge Davis.[3] This relieved us of much difficulty in formally opening our errand.

He came and reported to us that he had talked with Lincoln—and that Lincoln was not favorable to Cameron's appointment.

We finally had an interview with Lincoln ourselves. He was very much opposed to appointing Cameron, and expressed himself very emphatically in that direction.

Said he: "All through the campaign my friends have been calling me 'Honest Old Abe,' and I have been elected mainly on that cry. What will be thought now if the first thing I do is to appoint C., whose very name stinks in the nostrils of the people for his corruption?"

We came away without any very strong expectations of success. We were satisfied a good deal would have to be done after Mr. L. came here to Washington if it was accomplished.

I dont remember about the letter. I have an indistinct recollection that L. wished perhaps to see C. and have a plain talk with him about the objections which were urged against him &c.

CONVERSATION WITH GEN. CAMERON—FEB. 20TH 1875[4]

SENATOR C. SAID HE WOULD RENDER US WHATEVER ASSIStance was in his power. Said he had but few papers. By the way, he said, I have a number of important letters concerning my first going into the Cabinet of Mr. L. which I thought I would publish some time—I guess I had as well let you have them.

Lincoln sent for me by Swett—I told Swett I didn't want to go—and before I went I made Swett write it down what I was wanted for.[5]

Went and saw L. at Springfield [and] had two long conversations with him.[6] He told me he had made up his mind to give me either the Treasury or War Dept. he couldn't yet tell which. He said, before you go I will write you a letter saying that to you—and he did[7]

He said what about Seward? and seemed to be in doubt whether he would accept the State Dept which he had offered him. I replied you needn't hesitate on that score he will be sure to accept.

Afterwards Lincoln wrote me a letter saying he couldn't give me the Treasury but would give me something else.[8]

At Washington had a talk with him he asked me what I wanted—told him I didn't want anything. He might take the offices and keep them. I spoke pretty sharp. He offered to make me Atty. Genl. or give me the Interior. I told him I was no lawyer; I didn't want anything if he couldn't give me what he had offered. I had nothing to do with the final formation of the Cabinet.

Hamlin was for Welles.[9]

Didn't see the Rebel Com[missione]rs—the Sumter question was not absolutely decided in Cabinet—nothing was ever decided—there was general talk. Everybody understood Sumter was to be given up. Seward managed the matter with the Comrs. President told me that one or two of them complained about having been misled and deceived. How came the President to have so much faith in Lamon? Sent him to Va. & then to Charleston. When they fired on Sumter then I was for fight &c.

President and Chase sent for me to name some ment [men] at New York to make purchases &c.[10] I named Dix Governor Morgan and Alex.

Cummings.[11] I don't believe Cummings ever made any money out of contracts. I think Gov Morgan's brother did.[12]

It was necessary for somebody to go out and attend to Fremont.[13] Blair went first and came back and equivocated.[14] Then they all said I must go. I told Lincoln, I understand this—Fremont has got to be turned out, and somebody will have to bear the odium of it—if I go and do it I will probably lose my place here. In that case you must give me a foreign mission. That was the beginning of the Russian Mission.[15]

I went out and saw Fremont, and he said I am all ready now and I am expecting a great battle every day—you mustn't disturb me till after that. I talked the matter over with Wade and Chandler, and we decided to leave him there till he could make the contest he was ready for.[16]

Lincoln told me that he was more indebted to Judd than any other one man for his nomination, but I told him I thought Davis and Swett did more for him.[17] They bought all my men—Casey and Sanderson and the rest of them.[18] I was for Seward I knew I couldn't be nominated but I wanted a complimentary vote from my own State. But Davis and the rest of them stole all my men. Seward accused me of having cheated him.

Long before my report was written—sometime in September I think, I made a speech to Corcoran's Regiment out at Bladensburg—they had just come to Washington—in which I advocated the arming of negro troops.[19] The President was along and laughed with me over it on the way home. I think afterwards they persuaded him that I was going to try and set up as an opposition candidate to beat him next time

It was about a week after issuing [*the report*] he and Seward came down to Willards where Forney and I were and talked it over[20]—good-naturedly—Lincoln complained that it would hurt him in Kentucky—he was always afraid of Kentucky—he believed everything Speed told him about it. We didn't get any troops in Ky. Gen. —— made his camp up near the river and got his men from Indiana. We sent the men to the other camp farther toward the centre of the State.[21]

I wrote out the instructions to Gen. Sherman about furnishing arms to the negroes employed about the camp—the same instructions under which Hunter afterwards organized some negro regiments—I read the orders to Lincoln and he modified them in his own handwriting—to the effect that these orders shall not be construed to allow arms to be put into the hands of slaves &c.

When I went out of the cabinet Stanton annulled all my contracts and stopped enlistments—if they had let my arrangements go on I would have had a million of men under arms; we were organizing regiments as fast as we could supply them with arms. But when they stopped enlistments and annulled all my contracts the spirit of volunteering was checked and that necessitated their giving such unheard of bounties and finally they had to order a draft.[22] Chase was partly to blame for that because he was always scared about the finances.

When I went out of the Cabinet Lincoln asked me whom I wanted for my successor. I told him I wanted Stanton. Well said he go and ask Stanton whether he will take it. I started to go down and on the way I met Chase, and told him I was just going down to see Stanton—and told him what I was going for. No said he dont go to Stanton's office. Come with me to my office and send for Stanton to come there and we will talk it over together, and I did so.[23]

CONVERSATION WITH HON. N. B. JUDD
WASHINGTON FEB. 28 '76[24]

I CARRIED TO DOUGLAS LINCOLN'S CHALLENGE TO THE GREAT debate.

Lincoln came to my office in Chicago and asked my opinion about tendering Douglas a challenge of that kind. While he asked my advice he did it in such a way that (as I knew him so well) I saw that he had already decided the question for himself. I therefore without hesitation told him I thought it would be a good thing

He then sat down in my office and wrote that note. After I got the note I had very hard work to find Douglas. I hunted him for three days before I got a chance to present it to him.

When I did so finally it made him very angry—so much so that he almost insulted me. "What do you come to me with such a thing as this for?" he asked, and indulged in other equally ill-tempered remarks. Lincoln had meanwhile gone back to Springfield &c.

When Lincoln was going up to make his Freeport speech, Lincoln telegraphed to Peck and myself to meet him at Freeport. When we got there the evening before, we found that the committee had stopped him on his way out at Mendota, to bring him in next morning with the procession &c &c.

So we took the night train and went out to Mendota to meet him. We got there about two oclock at night, and we had Lincoln waked right up. We went up into his bed room, and had our talk with him there. He looked very comical sitting there on one side of his bed in his short night shirt, &c &c. He then read to us his answers to Douglas' Ottawa questions.

You remember they were concerning the Fugitive Slave law, and the abolition of Slavery in the District of Columbia &c. As we were up there in northern Illinois where the Anti-Slavery sentiment was very strong I insisted upon a slight change of the phraseology—not to make any material difference of the sense, but to make his declarations a little more palatable to the Republicans of that section. But I couldnt stir him. He listened very patiently to both Peck and myself, but he wouldn't budge an inch from his well studied formulas. "Now" said he "gentlemen, that is all. I wouldn't tomorrow mislead any gentleman in that audience to be made President of the U.S."

We went on down with him in the morning train, and he read his replies just as [he] had framed them himself, and as he had shown them to us.[25]

Always acted fairly with me

Wrote me the letter about Governorship

A great deal of fault was found at the time by the Whig press with Palmer, Cook, and myself about our stand in the election of Trumbull in 1854.[26] But Lincoln never joined in that clamor against us. He had the good sense to see that our course was the result of political sagacity. If we had voted for him, we should simply have been denounced by our own papers as renegades who had deserted the democrats and gone over to the Whigs. But in the course matters took that charge couldn't be maintained a moment against us. On the contrary we could maintain our entire consistency as anti-Nebraska Democrats, and that enabled us to carry over a fraction of the Democratic party sufficiently large to give us control of the State.

I remember in the winter of 1859 to have attended a legislative caucus in Springfield, the object of which was to labor to secure the nomination of Lincoln on the National ticket as Vice President.

When it came my turn to give my views, I strongly opposed this action, saying the proper and only thing to do was to claim the Presidency for him and nothing less.

After the Decatur Convention in 1860 Lincoln came to me to express his regret I had not been nominated [*for governor*]—he really decried—although to be entirely fair to his other friends he did not take sides one way or the other. We talked over the matter of appointing delegates to Chicago. I told him I had no influence in that Convention, but that if he had any desires in relation to the matter I would do my best to have them brought about. He then told me that he wished but one thing done, and that was that Judge Davis should be sent as one of the delegates. And, he added, "Judd you ought to go."

You remember we were both sent.

After the nomination at Chicago myself and ———— came down to Springfield with the Committee sent to notify Lincoln. While the Committee went on to the hotel to brush off the dust we jumped off at the junction and ran across to Mr. Lincoln's house where we found that Mrs. L. had spread out a lunch with champagne and liquors &c. I tell you I made her hustle those liquors out of there mighty fast, and by time the Committee [*arrived*] there was not a drop of anything to drink in sight &c &c.

When we came to get the Chicago Wigwam ready to be occupied by the convention I superintended the arrangements of the seats for the delegates on the stage. I put New York about the centre on the right hand side and grouped New England, Wisconsin, Minnesota, and all the strong Seward States immediately around her.

On the other side I put Illinois Pennsylvania (?) and Indiana, and Missouri, and grouped around these the delegates from the border States, and all the small doubtful delegations.

The advantage of the arrangement was, that when the active excitement and canvassing in the Convention came on, the Seward men couldn't get over among the doubtful delegations at all to log-roll with them, being absolutely hemmed in by their own followers who were not likely to be swerved from their set preference for Seward, &c &c

After Mr. Lincoln and the rest of us had all got here to Washington you remember there was active canvassing for a few days here about the formation of the first Cabinet. I recollect being very much excited and interested perhaps the very day before the inauguration, about a rumor I had heard that he had finally decided to take H. Winter Davis from Maryland instead of [*Montgomery*] Blair, and I and my democratic friends were very much alarmed at this lest it should make the Seward & Weed combination too strong for us, as we knew Judge Davis and Swett to be in that interest.[27]

I came down early next morning and was so lucky as to find Mr. Lincoln alone in the parlor. I began expressing my fears to him, when he turned round and said

"Judd, I told a man at eleven o'clock last night that if this slate broke again it would break at the head."

I replied "that is all I want to know. Good morning Mr. Lincoln."

I dont know whether you knew the fact that he showed his inaugural (which was printed at Springfield) to Old Man Blair.[28] He sent for me and said "can I go anywhere to get out of the way of these people for a while?" I said "Certainly come right to my room where you won't be disturbed."

So he came to my room and read his inaugural to Old man Blair, and took his suggestions on the subject—I dont know whether he made any corrections or changes at his instance or not. This was Sunday night.

Peace Convention.—Lincoln drafted the resolutions which the Legislature of Illinois passed to send Commissioners to Washington.

He asked a number there to go into the Senate one day, and also invited me, and read us that resolution, and asked our opinion as to the expediency of having it passed.

I took the ground that he couldn't afford to have the Legislature do that, until enough States had acted upon it to make it a success.

That course was finally agreed upon, and he handed the resolution over to Marshall (I think) and said "Marshall whenever Judd says the time has come put it in."[29]

CONVERSATION WITH HON. T. LYLE DICKEY (OF CHICAGO ILL) WASHINGTON OCT 20, 1876[30]

I MET MR. LINCOLN FIRST IN 1836. IN 1838 I HAD SOME CORrespondence with him. After 1839 our friendship became closer, and our co-operation in political matters (we were both Whigs) and our intercourse socially increased and continued until he was elected President—I meanwhile however having become separated from him in politics after the formation of the Republican party.

The first joint debate he held with Douglas was at Ottawa. Although my views of politics then differed from his—I and other old Whigs thinking Douglas ought to be returned to the Senate—though I was there on the platform at Ottawa as one of the avowed supporters of Douglas—yet when the meeting was over—along in the evening about twilight—he came up to my house (I was then living at Ottawa) and made my house his headquarters

I have no letters of his left—my office with all its books and papers—the accumulations of near a quarter of a century having been burned in 1864.

The most characteristic story I ever heard of Lincoln, was one I heard told by some man unknown to myself, one evening when I was waiting for the train, on a hotel porch at Centralia, Ill.

It was along in the summer of 1862 said the narrator, that the Republicans of the east became very intense in their pressure upon Lincoln to take some more decisive action than he had yet done in reference to the slavery question; and a certain class of radicals were forever reiterating the phrase that "the government must have a policy," &c. About this time the Bostonians sent down a delegation of their prominent men—some forty in number, (I think he said) to urge this view of his duty upon the President.

Lincoln received them cordially, and after the preliminary hand-shaking their spokesman, who had prepared himself for the occasion, began upon him with a long and formidable address. The President during the reading leaned over and listened to him with great apparent interest and attention, until at length he finished. When Lincoln saw that he was done, instead of beginning, as they all evidently expected, with a formal response, he straightened up a little in his chair, and throwing his leg across the corner of the table, and sat thinking for some minutes

Said he, finally:

"Do you remember that a few years ago Blondin walked across a tight rope stretched over the falls of Niagara?"

They said they did. He continued:

"Suppose that all the material values in this great country of ours, from the Atlantic to the Pacific—its wealth, its prosperity, its achievements in the present and its hopes for the future, could all have been concentrated, and given to Blondin to carry over that awful crossing and that their preservation should have depended upon his ability to somehow get them across to the other side—and suppose (addressing the spokesman) that everything you yourself held dearest in the world, the safety of your family, and the security of your home also depended upon his crossing, and suppose you had been standing upon the shore when he was going over, as he was carefully feeling his way along and balancing his pole with all his most delicate skill over the thundering cataract, would you have shouted to him 'Blondin, a step to the right!' 'Blondin, a step to the left!' or would you have stood there speechless, and held your breath and prayed to the Almighty to guide and help him safely through the trial?"

The delegation did not wait to hear the moral or the application of the story. They looked each other in the face for a moment, and then gathering up their hats and bidding the President good day passed silently out at the door

I spent a Sunday with him, I think in the fall of 1862; at any rate it was a while after the battle of Antietam and the campaign was again lagging. It was known that he had about made up his mind that McClellan would have to be removed. He didn't tell me so, but I was led to infer it from the fact that our conversation turned upon the skill and qualities of the various Generals in the field. Said he:

"Now there's Joe Hooker—he can fight—I think that point is pretty well established—but whether he can 'keep tavern' for a large army is not so sure."[31]

CONVERSATION WITH HON. HAMILTON FISH APRIL 10TH 1874[32]

BURNSIDE EXPEDITION

ABOUT THE TIME OF THE SAILING OF THE BURNSIDE EXPEDItion to Roanoke Island (?) Mr. Fish one day met Mr. Sumner going toward the White House, and learning from him that he was going merely to pay a social call, accompanied.[33] After duly paying their respects to Mrs. Lincoln and other ladies in the drawing-room, they sent their cards to the President in his office, who asked that they be shown up, and where some little time was spent in general talk. Finally Mr. Sumner began questioning the President about the Burnside expedition, the preparations for which it had of course been impossible to keep entirely secret, but whose destination was totally unknown to the public. "Well" said Mr. Lincoln "I am no military man, and of course, I cannot [know] all about these matters—and indeed if I did know, the interests of the public service require that I should not divulge them. "But" said he, rising and sweeping his long hand over a Map of the North Carolina coast which hung in a corner "Now see here. Here are a large number of inlets, and I should think a fleet might perhaps get in there somewhere. And if they were to get in here, dont you think our boys would be likely to cut some flip-flaps? I think they would."

Mr. Fish asked no more questions and adroitly turned the conversation. When they left the house Mr. Sumner expressed his impatience at the Presidents reticence. "Why" said Fish, "he told you where Burnside is going." "Oh," said Sumner "don't you think that was merely to put us off?" "You will see" rejoined Fish "the President was desirous of satisfying your curiosity so far as he could, but of course could not give you an official declaration on the subject. I think you ought to be well satisfied that he has been so frank. You will see by the result that he has correctly indicated the point of attack"

And so it turned out. But the direct and angular nature of Sumner had been utterly blind to the President's subtle hint, and so far from giving him credit for his confidence was going way exasperated at what he awkwardly mistook for an unobliging reserve.[34]

[CONVERSATION WITH HAMILTON FISH]
WASHINGTON MARCH 6 1874[35]

A T THE SUPREME COURT DINNER AT THE SECRETARY OF STATE'S last night, after the guests had retired to the library to smoke their cigars, Mr. Fish related the following incident with Prest Lincoln:

When the rebellion had been for some time in progress, the public sympathy and clamor in behalf of the Union prisoners in the south became so loud that it seemed necessary that something should be done in the premises. Secretary Stanton thereupon determined to appoint a commission consisting of Mr. Fish and Bishop Ames to proceed to Richmond and endeavor to effect an exchange.[36] Mr. Fish receiving a telegram to this purport in New York, came on and reported himself at the War Department. Stanton explained his wishes in detail to him stating that there were about an equal number (20,000) of Union prisoners in the south and rebel prisoners in the North, and that perhaps it would be better for both if they could be sent back.

At Stanton's request Fish and Ames spent a day or two at the War Department writing out instructions for themselves, and when they supposed they had them in proper shape Stanton took them over to Cabinet meeting for consideration. When he came back he did not appear to be pleased with the result. "I don't know" said he "how it is going to be. Mr. Seward raises objection that any exchange we may bring about on the basis of a cartel will be looked upon by the foreign powers as a *quasi* recognition and thus lead to dangerous complications."

Nevertheless the Commissioners having by this time themselves become interested in their work, felt disinclined to give the matter up, without further effort. They went and had a talk with Mr. Seward, who persisted in his opposition. And if they finally did go, he insisted they must on no account address either the Confederate President or other dignitaries by their pretended titles, but only as plain Mr. Jefferson Davis, &c &c.

Mr. Fish said he felt that negociation under such circumstances was practically impossible, and that they must find some means of modifying these very restrictive instructions. "Let us go and see Mr. Chase" said the Bishop. "It can do no possible good to go to Mr. Chase" said Fish in reply, "and we shall only have robbed him of so much time which he will desire to have given to his own troubles." "Well then let us go and see Mr. Lincoln." Mr. Lincoln was everybody's recource, and they went. They found the President alone, and sat down and rehearsed to him the story of their difficulties. As the details of the statement lengthened out in rather dry and tedious prolixity Mr. Lincoln settled back in his chair, gradually sliding down into a half reclining posture with his feet on a chair before him, and his slowly lengthening legs began to stretch out until Mr. Fish had serious apprehensions that they would go through the wall into the next room. His eyes closed themselves and he sat so still and motionless in self-thought, that his visitors having reached the end of their story thought surely they had been wasting their eloquence on a sleeping President.

Scarcely had the last word died away however, when they were undeceived. Opening his eyes the President straightened himself up, and showed them that he had not only heard but decided their petition while they were speaking, by replying in one of his characteristic illustrations: "Well Gentlemen, my opinion is, as that is a team that Stanton started out, he had better drive it through."

"That was all we wanted," continued Mr. Fish, "we went down to Richmond and in less than a week had arranged a cartel and an exchange of prisoners.

[*Later remark added to the text:*] This is a curious illustration of the untrustworthiness of all reminiscences. Bishop Ames & Mr. Fish had no such mission assigned to them.[37] Their duty was to relieve destitute Union prisoners—and this the rebel government did not permit them to do. They never got further than Fort Monroe.

CONVERSATION WITH EX-SENATOR FOSTER
OCT. 23 1878[38]

REMEMBERS THAT ON THE DAY CHASE WAS NOMINATED AND confirmed, being at the White House, and saying to the President

"Mr. President you sent us up a Chief Justice today, whom we confirmed at once. There had been so many contradictory reports and rumors that we had begun to have some doubts and anxieties on the subject Mr. Lincoln replied:

"Mr. Chase will make a very excellent judge if he devotes himself exclusively to the duties of his office, and dont meddle with politics.

"But if he keeps on with the notion that he is destined to be President of the United States, and which in my judgment he will never be, he will never acquire that fame and usefulness as a Chief Justice which he would otherwise certainly attain" &c

On another occasion (says Ex Senator Foster) I went early in the morning to ask Mr. Lincoln to suspend the execution of a soldier sentenced to be shot for desertion, the father of the man insisting that the offence was technical and not real:

"Why dont you men up there in Congress," replied the Prest. "repeal the law requiring men to be shot when they desert, instead of coming here to me, and asking me to override the law and practically make it a dead letter?"[39]

Mr. Foster answered that he had not asked the man's pardon, but only that the sentence should be stayed till the facts might be investigated, &c.

Said the Prest. "I shall grant your request. But you know that when I have once suspended the sentence of that man I can't afterwards order him to be shot."

CONVERSATION WITH HON LOT M. MORRILL OF M[AIN]E SEPT 20 1878[40]

I FIRST SAW MR. LINCOLN IN WASHINGTON IN 1861; HAD NO previous acquaintance with him; but had carefully followed and noted his contest with Douglas in 1858; and saw that he developed qualities and talents which at once marked him as a man of unusual power.

I was governor when Mr. Lincoln was nominated; my state was then in the hands of the Seward men; S. had been recognized as the leading interpreter of Republican ideas.

Fessenden was afraid of Seward;[41] I told him I was not for Seward for President; I didn't feel like trusting him in that place; and very naturally when it became necessary to make a choice I turned to Lincoln.

I went out to Chicago, though not as a delegate; was however called into council by the delegation. A Majority of our delegation was at first for Seward; but when it came to the critical point, and they had more fully consulted it was the other way

When I came to meet him here at Washington, and see and talk with him, I was more than ever convinced the people had made no mistake. I said to myself here are all the elements of character that go to make up a great man.

"I remember I went into his office one day—

"Well Governor" said he "jestingly, "who has been abusing me in the Senate today?"

I replied "Mr. President I hope not any of us abuse you knowingly & wilfully

"O well," said he "I don't mean that—personally you are all very kind—but I know we don't all agree as to what this administration should do, and how it ought to be done. And then our talk branched off on the general situation. Finally he said with great impressiveness:

I don't know but that God has created some one man great enough to comprehend the whole of this stupendous crisis and transaction from beginning to end, and endowed him with sufficient wisdom to manage and direct it. I confess I do not fully understand, and foresee it all. But I am placed here where I am obliged to the best of my poor ability to deal with it. And that being the case I can only go just as fast as I can see how to go."

—that was the way" continued Mr. Morill "he saw this thing as a stupendous movement, which he watched, and upon which he acted as he might best do when in his judgment the opportune moment came. I was satisfied he comprehended it as thoroughly as any man living could do. He saw that it was an immense affair; that in his dealings with it he must be backed by immense forces; and to this end it was his policy to hold the nation true to the general aim—to disregard petty deviations and delays—he saw the progress we made from time to time in its larger and more important aspects and relations—he moderated, guided, controlled or pushed ahead as he saw his opportunity—he was the great balance-wheel in short, that held the ship true to her course[42]

CONVERSATION WITH HON. LOT M. MORRILL, SEC OF TREASURY[43]

SAID MR. MORRILL,
I remember that at one time when I went into the room to President Lincoln, there were two women from Baltimore there who had come to try to obtain the release and parole of a prisoner of war who had been captured, and was then confined at Point Lookout. One of them was the mother of the young rebel, and after detailing his alleged sufferings, wound up her sympathetic appeals with the usual *finale* of such interviews, a copious shower of tears. At this point the president, who had patiently listened to the recital, asked casually when and how the boy had gone into the confederate service? The mother with evident pride, quickly responded with the whole history: he had gone south early in the war, served in such and such campaigns, made such and such marches, and survived such and such battles.

"And now that he is taken prisoner, *it is the first time*, probably, that you have ever shed tears over what your boy has done? asked the President with emphasis.

The question was so direct, and so completely described the true situation of affairs that the woman could frame no equivocation She sat dumb, and visibly convicted of her secession sympathies, by the very simple inquiry.

"Good morning Madam," said the President "I can do nothing for your boy today."

CONVERSATION WITH HON. WM. M. EVARTS, WASHINGTON OCT. 26 1876.[44]

(THIS AFTERNOON, IMMEDIATELY AFTER THE ADJOURNMENT of court while Mr. Evarts was gathering up his papers, I went to him and said "Mr. Evarts, I wish sometime when you are here waiting for a case to come on you would step into my office, and let me talk with you for an hour or so, about your recollection of and interviews with Mr. Lincoln.)

"Certainly," said he. I will do that with pleasure. You are at work upon his life I suppose. I had a very great respect for Mr. Lincoln. He and I were on most excellent terms. I really esteemed him very much. He was a man—he could see a point—he had a head on his shoulders—and nobody saw or acknowledged that more than Mr. Seward. If he (Mr. L.) had lived I should have had a much more responsible connection with the government than I had under Mr. Johnson. That is to say, I should at least have had the opportunity"

(I said to him, that I had been very much gratified with such allusions as he had made to President Lincoln in his public discourses.

"Yes" said he "I have always intended to treat him fairly. Mr. Adams fell into a very unfortunate error in making the statements he did concerning him,—or rather I should perhaps say in creating the impression he did by what he said.[45] Mr. Adams had gone abroad immediately after his inauguration, and remained abroad until after his death, and he was therefore not at all qualified to judge of him. Mr. Adams undoubtedly injured himself very much by his course

"I have always admired Mr. Lincoln. In my eulogy of Chase, I think it will be conceded that I said quite as much as I was justified in saying.

But I didn't abuse anybody else. When you are delivering a eulogy, eulogize your man, but it is not necessary to go out of your way to say harsh things of anybody else."

CONVERSATION WITH COL. W H LAMON
MARCH 10TH 1878.[46]

I T WAS IN 1863 BEFORE THE FALL OF VICKSBURG THAT THINGS were going very slow and the public mind was in very great suspense, and becoming very much prejudiced against Grant in consequence of his failure to reduce that stronghold. Nevertheless Lincoln held to his faith in him. Dickey had come in from the West and had giving [*given*] cheering reports in his behalf, and repeated his promises that Vicksburg should be taken by the 4th of July.

Wade went up to see the President and said to him—the people will not stand this state of affairs any longer. You must get rid of him.

Lincoln replied: I think I am about the only friend he has got left. Everybody says I must let him go. Even Washburne came and told me the other day he was afraid I would have to give him up.[47] But he has such and such chances and he has promised to take Vicksburg by the 4th of July, and I am for giving him the opportunity to redeem his promise. By the way Mr. Wade that reminds me of an anecdote—

(Wade interrupting angrily)

Yes Mr. President it is nothing but anecdotes. I have heard enough of them. You are letting the country go to h——l on anecdotes. We are not more than a mile from there now

(The President in turn interrupting with a twinkle of sardonic humor:)

Mr. Wade, that is just about the distance to the Capitol, isn't it?

(Wade seizes his hat and exit.) Going down the avenue he meets Kellogg.[48] "Where are you going?"

"Going up to see the President."

"Well I have just come from there—and think I made a d——d fool of myself too. Old Abe got off a good one on me, but I was so d——d mad that I was too blind to see it and it has just got through my wool. I believe I will go back with you and acknowledge the com.

(Goes back and the affair is laughed off.)[49]

CONVERSATION WITH HON LEONARD SWETT
OCT. 16 1878[50]

I REMEMBER GOING TO WASHINGTON DURING THE CAMPAIGN of 1864 when the prospect of the election looked very blue—nothing was being done.

I went into L's room and without ceremony or preliminary explanation, I asked him: Do you expect to be elected?

"Well," he replied "I dont think I ever heard of any man being elected to an office unless some one was for him."

CONVERSATION WITH HON LEONARD SWETT
MARCH 14, 1878[51]

I HAVE ALWAYS BEEN ANXIOUS TO KNOW WHEN THE FIRST Emancipation Proclamation was written. I was here at Washington and went up to the White House, about the 20th of August 1862.

Lincoln said to me: Come in here, Swett, I want to talk to you, and to hear your notions about some matters. Sit down here (this was in the morning at about 8 o'clock.) I want to show you certain documents that I have here.

He then went and brought out several bundles of letters which he opened.

First a dozen or more letters from Dana of the Tribune to the general effect that the President and all the men in the Administration were a sett of "wooden heads" who were doing nothing and letting the country go to the dogs[52]

"Now," said he, that represents one class of sentiment."

Next he read a long and ably written paper from Robert Dale Owen favoring a proclamation of emancipation.[53] Said Lincoln

"That is a very able paper indeed." He makes a very strong argument. I have written something on this subject myself. But it is not so able an argument as this."

Last he took up a letter from the Frenchman Gasparin, discussing, and very ably also, the various topics of the war from the standpoint of European nations.[54] If I remember aright he argued against a military emancipation, saying that the people of the old world were looking with great hope and solicitude to our example; and that they were very anxious that whatever changes came about should be the result of regular and not revolutionary measures.

After he had read all these papers Lincoln started out to discuss the proclamation or rather the question of issuing one. And we talked there till time for Cabinet meeting

"I had intended" said Mr. Lincoln to have shown you something else; but it has got so late I haven't time now."

I went away as the members of the Cabinet were coming in.

During the night I thought the interview over and made up my mind that from his having said that he had written something, and that that something was not as able an argument as Robert Dale Owen's—it couldn't be anything else than the proclamation itself

I went back next morning and hinted my surmises to him.

In answer he simply said with a significant smile: "Am I *doing* anything wrong?"

I replied "No, I can't say that you are."

"Well then," answered he banteringly "get out of here."[55]

CONVERSATION WITH HON. M. S. WILKINSON, MAY 22 1876.[56]

YOU CAME DOWN HERE ONE DAY AND SAID TO ME THAT THE President would like to see me on the next morning early.

It was at a time when the nomination of General Schofield for ——— was hanging fire in the Senate—it stood at the head of the list for a long time and every day it would be passed over without action[57]

The Missouri delegation in Congress at the time was all composed of Radicals, and they were bitterly opposed to Schofield on the ground that his administration tended to favor the opposing faction in Missouri politics, called "Claybanks." They thought Schofield was working against their interests, and they had been working with might and main to secure his removal.

The next morning just after breakfast I got on the cars to go up to the White House, and found Chandler on board. He also told me that the President had sent for him, though neither of us knew what he wanted with us.

We went in and Mr. Lincoln was there to receive us. He said to us, in substance:

"I suppose you gentlemen are opposed to the confirmation of General Schofield, in consequence of your dislike of his civil administration in Missouri. If so, that is what I want to talk with you about. Sherman says that Schofield will fight, and that he is a good soldier. Sherman says he would like to have him, and that he will give him a corps and put him at active duty in the field.[58]

Rosecrans ———

Now if you will confirm Schofield I will send him down there to Sherman and I will send Rosecrans up to take his place in Missouri

And I think that this will so harmonize matters that the whole thing will hang together.

That was all that was said

We went back to the Senate, making up our minds on the way that that was the best thing to be done.

As I have said Schofield's name was at the head of the Committee's list and as it had become the regular habit to pass it over, everybody expected that it would be done again that day. I sat by Chandler, and when the name was called he said "go ahead."

I thereupon got up, and said that up to that morning it had always been my intention to vote for his rejection, and told the Missouri delegation what my feelings were with reference to their controversy with him. But I also went on and told them that that morning I had had a talk with the President in the presence of Senator Chandler, and as I understood that General Sherman would like to have the services of Gen. Schofield in his department, and as the President had expressed his intention of supplying his place with a man who was understood to be acceptable to the Missouri people, I said that I should vote for his confirmation.

I recollect that Gratz Brown—who was the chief of the Missouri radicals sat near us, and although he had joined the church only a few weeks before, he was so taken by surprise when I began talking that he spoke out so that everybody on that side of the room could hear him "what in the h——l is up now?"[59] Ben. Wade also came round and said he wanted to understand all about this matter.

The result was that when Chandler and I had made our explanation Schofield was confirmed without difficulty—on[ly] the Missouri Senators (I think) voting in the negative.

CONVERSATION WITH HON. M. S. WILKINSON, MAY 23 1876[60]

I REMEMBER FOR INSTANCE, THAT DURING THE DARK DAYS IN 1862, during the time when President Lincoln used to tell us that when he got up in the morning it was his purpose and endeavor to do the very best he could and knew how *for that day*, not being able to foresee, or devise or determine what might be done, or what was best to be done for the morrow, that the Republican Senators used to meet almost every day in caucus, and by caucus conference decide upon the action they would take on pending legislation, so as to leave no chance for hesitation, or division, among themselves, but always to present a united and unbroken front to the Democratic opposition, and so as to furnish the public opinion of the North with no suspicion of division or doubt or despondency in the Republican councils

But it was not always fair sailing even in our Republican caucus. The Senators met in this way one morning when some grave and important measure (which I do not now remember) was about to come up for action. I recollect that on that occasion we were regaled by a long statement and speech from Mr. Collamer[61] to the effect that he had about made up his mind that the country would no longer endure the reverses, and the expenses and losses which had occurred. Mr. Fessenden followed in a similar strain. After him came Harris,[62] and then several others

Mr. Wade finally turned to Chandler and I and said "This is no place for us. The men who have already spoken, if they join their votes with the democrats can defeat the measure. If this kind of feeling is to prevail the question is decided against us." He rose up to go and we followed.

They called him back, and asked him why he was going. He repeated in a short address what he had said *sotte voce* to us. "From the talk I have already heard," said he "I see that this measure is beaten. Your votes gentlemen, if they agree with your talk will suffice with the help of the Democratic minority to kill the bill. There is no reason why we should stay. You can vote down the measure, and cripple the prosecution of the war, and bring about the ruin of the country—but I warn you that I shall demand the ayes and noes and that you shall go upon the record and take the full responsibility of your action."

We went out—there was a short session, and after it there was again a notice to meet in caucus. The fainthearts had canvassed the matter over, and when the discussion began it was altogether in a different tone and temper. The caucus unanimously resolved to put the measure through without delay; and next day the bill was passed Mr. Fessenden himself making the champion speech in its favor.[63]

CONVERSATION WITH GEN. S. A. HURLBUT, WASHINGTON MAY 4TH 1876. ABOUT MISSION TO CHARLESTON, MARCH 1861.[64]

IN THE LATTER PART OF MARCH MR. LINCOLN TOLD ME ONE day that Mr. Seward insisted that there was a strong Union party in the South—even in South Carolina. I told him that my advices from Mr.

Pettigrew and others were, that the secession element had absolute control—that there were no Union people there.[65]

He said he would like very much to know. I told him he could know—that I would go down there and find out for him. So in the course of a day or two Col. Ward H. Lamon and myself were sent down there—Lamon carrying some authority to call upon the Postmaster there, to settle his accounts, I think.

I had also suggested, from my knowledge of the country, a means of throwing men and supplies into Fort Sumter, and therefore took a simple letter of introduction from General Scott to Major Anderson, in case I should be able to get permission to go into the fort.[66]

I telegraphed in advance to my sister who was living in Charleston, that my wife and I would come to pay her a visit, as it was uncertain when we would have the opportunity of meeting again.

We arrived in Charleston on Saturday afternoon. On Sunday I saw a good many persons whom I had known before, and on Sunday evening went to Mr. Pettigrew's house, and was told by him, that there was no Union man in the city except himself—that is any man who declared himself a Union man.

On Monday I went to see Governor Pickens and asked him to let me go to the islands around Fort Sumter to see some old comrades of mine who were there in the fortifications which were being erected, but which he refused.[67]

I saw two or three representative men of each class among lawyers, merchants, mechanics, and northern citizens settled there, and found only one expression among them all: and that was that there would be no war—that the north dared not or would not fight—and that secession would establish the city of Charleston as the great commercial metropolis of the South.

The object of my mission was accomplished, and I left Charleston on Monday night, returned to Washington, and made my report to the President verbally, which he caused me to repeat in the presence of Mr. Seward. Seward still insisted upon it that there was a strong Union party in the South which would stop the movement. I told him that Fort Sumter at that time was commanded by batteries which had been erected without molestation, and that I was satisfied from my knowledge of the men that it was the intention to reduce the fort at all hazards.

The President asked me to make a written report which I did elaborately, and which he read to the Cabinet—at least he told me he did. The next day I went to bid him good bye. He asked me what I was going for. I told him I was going home to put Illinois on a war footing. These events occurred about ten days before the firing on Fort Sumter.

I had known Mr. Pettigrew ever since I was a boy—I had read law in his office for four years. He had written me about the situation of affairs there, after Mr. Lincoln's election.

He was at that time the best lawyer in the South, and the strongest man in the State, as far as character, ability and purity went, and never surrendered his Union convictions nor disguised them. He was, I think, employed by the State in codifying the laws—I think they did not even take that away from him.

Mr. Lincoln felt doubtful—but he evidently thought they would not have proceeded to the extent to which they had, if they had not intended to carry things to extremity.

Lamon went to see the Postmaster, and I think he was offered permission to go to the fort. He stopped at the Charleston Hotel and there was a good deal of curiosity manifested as to what he came for since he represented the government. I was a private citizen merely and didn't represent anybody

My interview with Governor Pickens was simply to ask permission to go to the islands.

There was no mistaking the entire unanimity and earnestness of the secession sentiment.

There were hundreds of men delicately brought up, who never had done a day's work in their lives, yet who were out there on those islands throwing up entrenchments.

The fire eating part of the population was for a fight in any event—the business men were for a fight as a business man here, because they said dissolution would insure the business supremacy of the city of Charleston in the Southern Confederacy.

CONVERSATION WITH HON. LYMAN TRUMBULL[68]

SEWARD IN CONDUCT OF FOREIGN AFFAIRS HAS ACTED WITH-
out

Spoke for the Admn. without consulting the President

Seward given to undertaking the control of the whole Admn.

Interfering with the War Dept.

Given to assuming authority

Stanton never allowed it

Seward assumed a good deal of jurisdiction

My recollection is in some correspondence he had carried on without consulting the President.

I think Mr. Lincoln said in that conversation he would see all the dispatches himself[69]

CONVERSATION WITH HON. J. P. USHER, WASHINGTON OCT. 11TH 1877.[70]

IT WAS NOT GENERALLY KNOWN AT THE TIME THAT MR. SEWARD and the President had gone down to the Hampton Roads Conference.[71] Stanton probably knew it, but I did not, and I dont think the other members of the Cabinet did, except Blair perhaps.

After the fact became public through the newspapers, Otto came home one day and reported a conversation he had had with Schenck at the Club room or somewhere.[72] Schenck was very violent—spoke in the most bitter and denunciatory terms of Seward and said he hoped the rebels would catch him and put him in Libby prison.[73] Otto was very much astonished at the violence of the language and so expressed himself at the time.

After they came back, and it became known what had transpired at the conference, Otto meet Schenck again and said to him "I suppose now General, you have changed your mind.

No said he, he had not. Seward was a d——d —— he ought to be caught and put in Libby.

When Lincoln brought forward that compensation message (a few days after the Conference) in Cabinet, I remembered what Schenck had said.[74] I then thought, that if he should send that message to Congress, extreme and radical men of the character of Schenck would make it the occasion of a violent assault on the President and perhaps thus weaken his influence to procure men and money to prosecute the war.

I believe if I had then said "I do approve of this message and measure, and will sustain you in it"—he would have sent it to Congress. I think his heart was so fully enlisted in behalf of such a plan that he would have followed it if only a single member of his Cabinet had supported him in the project.

As it was he only sighed and said in his sad manner, "You are all against me."[75]

He said, "how long has this war lasted, and how long do you suppose it will still last?" "We cannot hope that it will end in less than a hundred days. We are now spending three millions a day, and that will equal the full amount I propose to pay, to say nothing of the lives lost and property destroyed. I look upon it as a measure of strict and simple economy."

But he received no encouragement and simply brought a long sigh and said "You are all against me."

(Q. How long was the matter discussed?)

The discussion of the whole matter didn't last ten minutes. The reason he put forward was "How long will the war last?" And then proceeding as if in answer to himself "at least a hundred days. We are spending three millions a day, besides all the blood which will be shed."

Seward was not there. He would probably have approved the measure—the rest were I think all there.

It was about five days after the Hampton Roads Conference.

CONVERSATION WITH HON. J. P USHER, WASH[INGTO]N OCT 8, 1878.[76]

WHEN THE PRESIDENT WAS ABOUT TO SIGN THE FINAL Emancipation Proclamation, (Jan. 1st 1863) Mr. Blair called his attention to the excepted parishes in L[*ouisian*]a and urged that inasmuch as the excepted territory was but a drop in the bucket, and as this was destined to be read as a great historical document, it was a pity [*to*] have its unity, completeness, and direct simplicity marred by such a trifle of detail, which after all was more a matter of form than anything else, especially since the legal effect of the exception would be practically obliterated; and Mr. Seward joined in the suggestion.

"Well," said the President, "I promised Bouligny if they would go on and hold an election down there and send up members, I would accept and recognize them."[77]

"If you have made that promise" answered Blair, of course I do not wish you to break or violate it."

Here Chase chimed in saying that as yet they were not here, and Congress had never signified its willingness to admit such members—in point of fact there was every reason to believe it would absolutely refuse to admit them, and would insist that these States were by the act of rebellion out of the Union and not entitled to have their representatives received or acknowledged.

Mr. Lincoln was walking across the floor, and suddenly stopping about midway of the room turned his head half-round and looked at Chase:—

"Then I am to be bullied by Congress am I?"

"I'll be d——d if I will."[78]

CONVERSATION WITH HON. H. HAMLIN
APL. 8 1879[79]

I T IS A SOURCE OF GREAT GRATIFICATION TO ME THAT MY RElations with Mr. Lincoln were not only those of uninterrupted friendship, but those of entire harmony and intimate and unreserved cordiality. It had come down to me as a sort of tradition that in the whole history of the country there had been only one instance in which the President and Vice President had not been under more or less estrangement—that between Mr. Van Buren and Johnson.[80] I made up my mind that in my case no such estrangement should exist, and kept that resolution.

There is a popular impression that the Vice President is in reality the second officer of the government not only in rank but also in power and influence. This is a mistake. In the early days of the republic he was in some sort an heir apparent to the Presidency. But that is changed. He presides over the Senate—he has a casting vote in case of a tie—and he appoints his own private secretary. But this gives him no power to wield, and no influence to exert. Every member who has a constituency, and every Senator who represents a state, counts for more in his own locality, and with the Executive who must needs, in wielding the functions of his office, gather around him, and retain by his favors those who can vote in Congress and can operate directly upon public sentiment in their houses.

I saw very soon, that the V. P. was a nullity in W[ashingto]n and recognizing that fact I abstained from any effort to absorb duties or functions not my own. I did not obtrude upon or interfere with the Presidential duties, though I always gave Mr. [Lincoln] my views, and when asked, my advice. His treatment of me was on his part that of kindness and consideration, and my counsels had all the more weight with him, that he thus practically knew them to be disinterested and free from any taint of intrigue or factional purpose.

CONVERSATION WITH HON. J. HOLT
WASHINGTON OCT 29 1875[81]

I ASKED JUDGE HOLT, WHETHER THE RECORDS OF COURTS Martial, preserved in the Bureau of Military Justice were in such a condition as to make it possible to find the cases on which President Lincoln had made autograph memoranda and orders?)

There is, said Judge H. such a mass of these cases (reaching as high as 30,000 a year during the war) that it would be next to impossible to find them unless we knew what particular case to look for under the name &c of the party tried.

You of course remember the class of cases the President used to call his "leg cases"—i.e. sentences of death for desertion, or misbehavior in face of the enemy &c &c. He was always very loth to act on these, and sometimes kept them a long while before disposing of them, which was generally by commuting the sentence to imprisonment at hard labor &c.

I used to try and argue the necessity of confirming and executing these sentences. I said to him, if you punish desertion and misbehavior by death, these men will feel that they are placed between two dangers and of the two they will choose the least. They will say to themselves, there is the battle in front where they may be killed, it is true, but from which they also have a good chance to escape alive; while they will know that if they fly to the rear their cowardice will be punished by certain death.

To all which the President would reply: Yes, your reasons are all very good, but I don't think I can do it. I don't believe it will make a man any better to shoot him, while if we keep him alive, we may at least get some work out of him. You have no doubt, continued he, heard the story of the soldier who was caught and asked why he had deserted. "Well, Captain," said the man, "it was not my fault. I have got just as brave a heart as Julius Cesar but these legs of mine will always run away with me when the battle begins." I have no doubt that is true of many a man who honestly meant to do his duty but who was overcome by a physical fear greater than his will. These came to be familiarly known between us as his "leg cases."[82]

(In these cases when they were brought to the President's knowledge he always promptly telegraphed that the execution of the sentence should be suspended, and the record sent to him. In the press of business large numbers of them accumulated in one of the pigeon holes of his desk)

The President would call me to go over them with him—occupying hours at a time. He was free and communicative in his criticism and comment on them, and his true nature showed itself in these interviews. He shrank with evident pain from even the idea of shedding human blood. (In a great army like ours these cases came by hundreds, and the carrying out of all these many sentences impressed him as nothing short of "wholesale butchery.") In every case he always leaned to the side of mercy. His constant desire was to save life. There was only one class of crimes I always found him prompt to punish—a crime which occurs more or less frequently about all armies—namely, outrages upon women. He never hesitated to approve the sentences in these cases. This was the only class of cases I can now recall in which he was unhesitating in his action[83]

There was one other case in which the President promptly approved the finding and sentence of the Court Martial. That was in the trial and conviction of Fitz John Porter[84]

The record in that case came up through my office and I made my report upon the testimony and trial. When I was reading my report to him and presenting a summary of the evidence showing the conduct of Porter on that occasion—that he heard and recognized from the sound of the cannon that the battle was going against Pope

"Why certainly," said the President "I was standing out here in this yard that afternoon, and could hear the sound of the cannon here, and I knew it myself."

McDowell's testimony in that case was very damaging to Porter, and both he and his friends saw and felt the crushing force of it as it came out on the trial[85]

"You will put your force in here to the left" said McDowell to Porter, on the day of battle.

"But if I get in there I shall get into a fight," said Porter.

"Gen. Porter I thought that was what we came out here for" rejoined McDowell, and wheeling his horse spurred away to his command. It was perhaps as withering a rebuke given in quiet words as was ever uttered

Senator Chandler in a speech on the subject brought out a fact which had also come to my knowledge from another source, that Porter himself admitted that he had "not been true to Pope."

It was late at night after McDowell's testimony had been given, that Porter was in the room of the stenographer waiting for a transcript of the evidence, that he uttered the language. I have a written report of the fact by one of the men who heard him. He was pacing up and down the room, entirely absorbed in his own reflections, and not evidently addressing any one, but, as men sometimes do, thinking aloud—that he said—

"It is a fact—I was not true to Pope, but I was true to McClellan."

All the testimony which we have got from rebel sources confirms the judgment of all fair critics that Porter had no cause whatever for his inaction. For instance he alleged that he saw at a certain hour of the day great clouds of dust in the direction in which he would have been obliged to go, which made it necessary for him to remain where he was lest he should run into the hands of an overwhelming rebel force.

Now it turns out from a letter found in the rebel archives, written by J. E. B. Stuart the cavalry raider, that he created all this dust expressly by having a few of his men tie brush to their horses' tails and ride them up and down the main road, on purpose to deceive Porter.[86]

CONVERSATION WITH HOLT, APL. 2 1874.[87]

SPEAKING OF THE ANONYMOUS THREATS WHICH WERE SOME-times written to the President and his too great heedlessness of them Judge Holt says:)

When his friends spoke to him on the subject and urged him to take greater precautions he used to answer them by means of an illustration drawn from his early life and experience in the Western country.

"What is the use" he would say "of putting up the bars when the fence is down all around?"

When Judge Holt went into the war Department, he found from the records that Slidell had appointed one brother-in-law to Annapolis; and one to [command] West Point (Beauregard) over the head of five or six Captains deserving the promotion.[88] The outrage was so flagrant that Holt immediately and without even consulting the Prest. revoked the orders and appointed (Capt Delafield).[89] When Slidell (always insolent and overbearing) became aware of it he grew furious, and wrote a note to Buchanan, demanding to know whether it had been done by his authority.

Holt went over to Cabinet meeting—there but Stanton and one or two others present—and Buchanan, without saying a word handed him Slidell's note. Holts ire rose to fever heat on the instant.

"Mr. President," said he "I think we have heard the crack of the slave-drivers lash over our heads about long enough. He knew as well as we do when he penned that note that I cannot do an act or issue a single order except by and through your authority and that it was an outrage to ask the question. It is either your act or it is nothing at all."

"That is true" said Buchanan "and I will write him a note and tell him so."

"Mr. President," replied Holt, "you must do more; you must write and distinctly tell him that it was your own act."

"Well" said he "I will," (— and Holt is under impression that he did.

While Holt was yet in the War Department before Mr Cameron took it, Mr. Lincoln one day sent for him and taking him into a side room, asked him, whether in his communications with Maj. Anderson any suspicion or doubt had ever arisen in his mind as to his loyalty or firmness. Mr. Holt replied that he had never had any such doubt, at which Prest. Lincoln expressed himself much gratified, and the matter was not pursued further.

CASS' RESIGNATION

After the final development of the treason in Buchanan's Cabinet, which forced Cass to resign his place as Secretary of State, Holt, who had been on intimate terms with him went to him to learn whether his resignation was indeed true and whether his determination were irrevocable.[90]

Cass confirmed with his own lips the rumor Holt had heard; saying that representing the northern and loyal constituency which he did, he could no longer, without dishonor to himself and to them remain in such treasonable surroundings. Holt endeavored to persuade him that under the circumstances it was all the more necessary, that the loyal members of the Cabinet should remain at their posts, in order to prevent the countrys passing into the hands of the secessionists by mere default.

But Cass replied no; that the public feeling and sentiment of his section would not tolerate such a policy on his part. "For you" he said, "coming from a border state, where a modified, perhaps a divided public sentiment exists, that is not only a possible course but it is the true one;

it is your duty to remain, to sustain the Executive, and to counteract the plots of the traitors. But my duty is otherwise I must adhere to my resignation."[91]

BLACK'S LOYALTY
CONVERSATION WITH HOLT, APL 1874[92]

Notwithstanding the fact that judge black gave Buchanan his written opinion as Atty Genl that though Secession was unlawful the Constitution gave the Prest. no power to coerce the States, Judge Black remained loyal in his feelings and actively and earnestly labored to prevent the dismemberment of the Union, while he remained in Buchanan's Cabinet.—[93]

"BUCHANAN AND THE FEB. 22 PARADE"
CONVERSATION WITH HON. J. HOLT
MAY 30TH, 1877.[94]

My impression is mr. stanton came to me very late at night—it must have been near midnight—and that he was very earnest in his desire to have me consent to take the War Department.

There was something very pressing in his anxiety—there was also in that of Mr. Black, whom I saw next day. My impression now is that there seemed to be the feeling in both their action and speech indicating an important crisis—that something had occurred—and that they wanted a man whose views they knew and could rely on—that they were laboring under grave apprehensions, etc.

My impression is that I went in on Monday morning and that this matter had all been arranged on the evening before.

I suppose you know when I came to be subsequently nominated and confirmed. It was the result of bullying on the part of Mr. Slidell. He was especially bitter toward me. He introduced a resolution into the Senate to inquire by what authority the President appointed a Secretary of War ad interim. In the course of the debate, he said it was very well known that if I was nominated in the Senate, I would not be confirmed. Now, the President had offered to nominate me; but I had said to him that I didn't care about it, that I could serve him just as well for the short time the administration had yet to run. But when I saw what Mr. Slidell had said, I went up next day, taking the paper in my hand that contained his remarks, and told the President now that he might send my name to the Senate. He said he would send it up at once and did see that I was confirmed without any hesitation or delay whatever. All the Reps voted for the confirmation, I believe.

The sailing of the Star of the West was attempted to be countermanded because we had received a dispatch from Major Anderson giving notice of the erection of a battery among the sandhills. But the vessel had sailed.[95]

Early in the war, I made an address before a camp of soldiers in Indiana—I think that was soon after I had made a similar one in Kentucky. Afterwards, I made one in Boston and I think in New York.

Mr. Cobb had been distinguished as a popular speaker.[96] In social intercourse, he was particularly noted for his apparent frivolity, his wit, and fund of anecdotes. He was a man of infinite talk and amusement. Cobb always let himself out in a cabinet meeting—always set the cabinet in a roar whenever he was there. And yet, under this, I think, he was in his heart a bitter, vindictive man. I think his hatred of the North was terrible. In that respect, he was almost the equal of Toombs.[97]

I happened to meet Toombs once when the difficulty between the North and South first was prominent and, as was the case then, that everybody at once went to talking about it. On that occasion, he seemed animated by an almost fiendish malignancy. ——— said he: "If I were to die tomorrow, I should care to have but one epitaph cut in my tombstone: 'Here lies the man who destroyed the Republic of the U.S.'"

I think Cobb came very near up to that standard. I think I never encountered a more bitter and malignant hatred for the Union or the North than in him.

Thompson was not a man of any marked ability, though he was a very ambitious man.[98]

Floyd also struck me as a man who was very different from the others.

The others were both open and unreserved in their hostility to the government. But [he] always kept up a show of loyalty and never broke off into open adhesion of the rebels until the affair of the trust bonds came out on him.[99] I think he was not a sincere man. He always in our intercourse professed to be very friendly to me; and yet I afterwards learned from a gentleman in whom I had every reason to have confidence that he at other times used language showing a very great hostility to me.

I went myself to Mr. Cass when I found he was going to retire, expressing my regret and my conviction that he ought to stay and prevent the advent of a more dangerous man in his place. I remember I was myself greatly excited about the matter, for it seemed to me the beginning of a general disintegration of the cabinet. I think his withdrawal was more the result of his very great age as well as his personal timidity and particularly his sensitiveness of public opinion. I think he was very much influenced by his apprehension of public censure. Said he, "It was impossible to stand up before my people (meaning the North thereby) and remain in the cabinet of Mr. Buchanan."

I said to him, "Where then does it stand with me? What shall I do?"

Said he, "You are in a totally different position. You are perfectly right in remaining in the cabinet and doing your best to maintain and uphold the government."

I think it was his great dread of public opinion which he felt he could not endure by staying in.

"I think the battery of flying artillery we finally got here was a great means of saving the City of Washington. We had very great difficulty in getting the President's consent to have it appear on the street, and its presence become known to the people, which was one of the great objects we had in view. But the President was very much afraid to have this done because he very much desired to keep out of view everything like military demonstration, particularly during the sessions of the Peace Convention, which was then convened here. This weakness too, I am satisfied grew much more out of the Presidents infirmities and age than anything else.

We finally, however, succeeded in getting the battery to show itself on the avenue on the occasion of the parade on the 22d of February, which he countermanded once, as I have already told you. The troops had a good effect and in particular this battery, which was a showy, dashing corps, and I think made such an impression on the public feeling here that after that the conspirators gave up their plan of making any attempt on the city while they remained.

The President's [   ] and dilatory policy was, I think, in a very large measure the result of his age infirmities.

He could not, apparently, bear up under the pressure these Southern men were constantly bringing on him. He was at times so despondent that it seemed as if he could not look those men in the face.

I know I used myself to have very great pity for the President. I used sometimes to go to him early in the morning when he would look as pale and haggard and worn out as if he had been tramping on a treadmill all night.

This utter despondency of his was well known among all his friends. He was frequently known to say that he believed that he would be the last President of the U.S. even if he felt that it was an imprudent thing to say, but it seemed as if he could not [   ]

Under [   ] feelings as this, those Southern fellows used to come around him and browbeat him. Perhaps the most insolent of all, however, was Mr. Slidell. It was at times almost unbearable to see him rush in and, with domineering manner and blustering voice and the language of an overseer, browbeat the President.

The incident of Slidell's finally breaking with the President was as follows: When I went into the War Department, I found that Floyd had put Beauregard, who was a relative of Slidell's, as Superintendent of West Point, over the heads of at least half a dozen officers who were all better entitled to the place, both by reason of seniority and superior services. I, of course, revoked the assignment. When Slidell heard of this, he was in a great rage and wrote the President a very curt note, asking whether this had been done by his orders. Mr. Buchanan sent the note to me.

I went to him with the note in my hand—my impression was that Mr. Stanton was sitting at the other end of the table—I said to the President: "I think we have had enough of this sort of thing. This sounds altogether to me like the crack of an overseer's whip. It is a piece of the absolute insolence in him to ask such a question. Of course, I understand, Mr. President, that everything I do is by your authority—every act I do and every order I make is for you alone and not for myself. I am but your agent and officer and exercise no power or authority of my own whatever."

"Certainly," said Mr. Buchanan, "I will write him that I endorse and sustain the act."

Said I, "Mr. President, I must ask you to do more. I must ask you to address him and say that this was your own order."

And the President did it, and that broke up their intercourse entirely.

About the time the Sumter matter was under discussion, while the commissioners were here awaiting their answer about the cabinet meeting of which Mr. Black speaks (Dec. 29), Mr. Black himself had made a very earnest and eloquent appeal to the President to sustain Anderson.

He said to him, with perhaps as much earnestness as a man ever puts into his words: "Mr. President, I will serve you to the utmost and everything save one—I will not dishonor myself."

THE INTERVIEW BETWEEN THAD. STEVENS & MR. LINCOLN AS RELATED BY COL R. M HOE.[100]

SHORTLY BEFORE THE ELECTION OF 1864 COL. R. M. HOE OF N.Y happened to be in company with Hon. S. Cameron and Hon. Thad. Stevens of P[ennsylvani]a when they went one evening to call on the President, and being there, by request of the parties remained present at what turned out to be a very noteworthy interview.)

Some preliminary business having been transacted, Mr. Stevens introduced the main topic of the evening:

"Mr. President," said he "our Convention at Baltimore has nominated you again, and, not only that, but we are going to elect you. But the certainty of that will depend very much on the vote we can give you in P[*ennsylvani*]a in October; and in order that we may be able in our State to go to work with a good will we want you to make us one promise; namely that you will reorganize your Cabinet and leave Montgomery Blair out of it."

Mr. Stevens then went on to elaborate his reasons, and a running fire of criticism [*and*] of comment was entered upon between the three gentlemen gradually rising in warmth and interest, the whole interview lasting some two or three hours. As the discussion proceeded, Mr. Lincoln rose from his seat and walked up and down the room.

The issue being made up the President finally gave his answer, in substance as follows, towering up to his full height, and delivering his words with emphatic gestures, and intense earnestness of speech:

"Mr. Stevens, I am sorry to be compelled to deny your request to make such a promise. If I were even myself inclined to make it, I have no right to do so. What right have I to promise you to remove Mr. Blair, and not make a similar promise to any other gentleman of influence to remove any other member of my cabinet whom he does not happen to like? The Republican party, wisely or unwisely has made me their nominee for President, without asking any such pledge at my hands. Is it proper that you should demand it, representing only a portion of that great party? Has it come to this that the voters of this country are asked to elect a man to be President—to be the Executive—to administer the government, and yet that this man is to have no will or discretion of his own. Am I to be the mere puppet of power—to have my constitutional advisers selected for me beforehand, to be told I must do this or leave that undone? It would be degrading to my manhood to consent to any such bargain—I was about to say it is equally degrading to your manhood to ask it.

"I confess that I desire to be re-elected. God knows I do not want the labor and responsibility of the office for another four years. But I have the common pride of humanity to wish my past four years Administration endorsed; and besides I honestly believe that I can better serve the nation in its need and peril than any new man could possibly do. I want to finish this job of putting down the rebellion, and restoring peace and prosperity to the country. But I would have the courage to refuse the office rather than accept it on such disgraceful terms, as not really to be the President after I am elected."[101]

CONVERSATION WITH HON. JOHN SHERMAN OCT. 10TH 1878[102]

DURING THE WEEK OR TEN DAYS PRECEDING THE INAUGURA-tion there was much talk and speculation about the coming cabinet.

Chase had been understood to have accepted the Treasury. But after Lincoln came to Washington there seemed to be some hitch or hesitancy about the matter.

Blair sent to me to ask if I would [*accept*] a place in the Cabinet. I also understood that Chase suggested that in case he didn't take the Treasury he would like to see an Ohio man have it, and preferred me.

I am pretty sure that Lincoln was talked to about the matter

I also heard that Seward said that he favored that combination—that Seward was for me and against Chase.

Lincoln never mentioned the matter to me—in fact I never had any talk of a political nature with him till after the inauguration.

Neither did I ever talk to Chase about it—though I knew he was friendly to me, and understood that he at one time at least favored this arrangement. At least I got the impression that Chase seemed to be favorable to it and that he hesitated about resigning his place in the Senate to which he had just been elected.

Weed too favored taking me—he was the friend of Mr. Seward and it was understood that it would please Seward.[103]

You will remember that I had been a member of the House; that I had held a somewhat prominent place during the stormy Kansas times—that I had been the candidate for Speaker in the contest of ——— [*1859*]; and then was sent out to Kansas as one of that investigating committee.[104] I suppose I should have been made Speaker—that I had the best chance. But when it was understood that Chase had been tendered a Cabinet appointment, and would probably accept my friends wrote to me from Ohio asking me to become a candidate for the Senate in his place. I preferred this to the Speakership. I and my friends found, on canvassing the Legislature that my chances would be good. I found too that Chase was in my favor. He told me that if he went into the Cabinet, as he then thought he would do, he would like to see me come to the Senate in his place.

Frank Blair, then the most prominent man in Missouri, went out to Kansas with us.[105] We were together there a great deal—as well as in the House. In that way here in Washington I became well acquainted with the Blair family. Used to dine at Montgomery's very often.

After Lincoln came to Washington, Chase hesitated—he disliked to give up the Senate as much as he disliked to give up the Presidency. It was then that some one came to me from Frank Blair, I think to ask me if I would go into the Cabinet. It was argued too that Lincoln was making a mistake in taking so many Presidential rivals, and especially so many old men into his Cabinet—that he needed younger, more active, and more unselfishly devoted men to be his lieutenants in such stormy times.

I replied that I could not consent—I could not stand in Chase's way, and that I greatly preferred that he should go into the Cabinet, and I come to the Senate in his place &c &c &c.

CONVERSATION WITH HON JAS SPEED
WASHINGTON FEBY 11 1876[106]

IT IS EXTREMELY DIFFICULT (SAID MR. S.) TO ADEQUATELY portray in writing the exquisite pathos of Mr. Lincolns character as manifested in his action from time to time.

There was the incident of granting a discharge to the woman's sons.

"Is that all?" he asked of Edward, the usher, after the usual multitude of daily visitors had entered and presented their requests, petitions or grievances.[107]

"There is one poor woman there yet Mr. President" replied Edward. She has been here for several days, and has been crying and taking on—and hasn't got a chance to come in yet.

"Let her in," said Mr. L.

The woman came in and told her story. It was just after the battle of Gettysburg. She had a husband and two sons in the army, and she was left alone to fight the hard battle of life. At first her husband had regularly sent her a part of his pay and she had managed to live. But gradually he had yielded to the temptations of camp life and no more remittances came. Her boys had become scattered among the various armies, and she was without help, &c. &c. Would not the President discharge one of them that he might come home to her?

While the pathetic recital was going on the President stood before the fire-place, his hands crossed behind his back, and his head bent in earnest thought. When the woman ended and waited a moment for his reply his lips opened and he spoke—not indeed as if he were replying to what she had said, but rather as if he were in abstracted and unconscious self-communion:

"I have two, and you have none."

That was all he said. Then he walked across to his writing table, at which he habitually sat, and taking a blank card, wrote upon it an order for the son's discharge—and upon another paper he wrote out in great detail where she should present it—to what Department, at what office and to what official giving her such direction that she might personally follow the red tape labyrinth.

A few days later, at a similar close of the "general reception" for the day, Edward said "That woman, Mr. President, is here again, and still crying."

"Let her in" said L. "What can the matter be now."

Once more he stood up in the same place before the fire, and for the second time heard her story. The Presidents card had been like a magic passport to her. It had opened forbidden doors, and softened the sternness of official countenances. By its help she had found headquarters—camp—Regiment, and company. But instead of giving a mother's embrace to a lost son restored, she had arrived only in time to follow him to the grave. The battle at Gettysburg—his wounds—his death at the hospital—the story came in eloquent fragments through her illy-stifled sobs. And now would not the President give her the next one of her boys?

Once more Mr. Lincoln responded with sententious curtness as if talking to himself. "I have two and you have none"—a sharp and rather stern compression of his lips marking the struggle between official duty and human sympathy. Then he again walked to his little writing table and took up his pen to write for the second time an order which should give the pleading woman one of her remaining boys. And the woman, as if moved by a filial impulse she could not restrain moved after him and stood by him at the table as he wrote, and with the fond familiarity of a mother placed her hand upon the Presidents head and smoothed down his wandering and tangled hair. Human grief and human sympathy had overleaped all the barriers of formality, and the ruler of a great nation was truly the servant, friend and protector of the humble woman clothed for the moment with a paramount claim of loyal sacrifice. The order was written and signed, the President rose and thrust it into her hand with the choking ejaculation "There!" and hurried from the room, followed, so long as he could hear, by the thanks and blessings of an overjoyed mother's heart. The spoken words of the scene were few and common-place; but a volume could not describe the deep suppressed emotion or the simple pathetic eloquence of the act.[108]

CONVERSATION FEB. 20TH 1873
EX M[EMBER OF] C[ONGRESS] ORTH OF IND[IANA][109]

REMEMBERS WHEN HON. J. K. DUBOIS OF ILL. CAME TO Springfield, determined to get a place in Lincoln's Cabinet. Orth went to Prest on his behalf. "Well you see" said he "I like Uncle Jesse very much, but I must do something for this great Methodist Church. There's Seward [who] is an Episcopalian, Chase is an Episcopalian, Bates is an Episcopalian, and Stanton swears enough to be one. Of course until the matter was brought to my attention I didn't know anything about the churches to which my cabinet belonged. But in this way I have without any intention whatever in the matter selected them all from a single church &c &c &c.

CONVERSATION WITH REV. E D NEILL, IN MY OFFICE AT WASH[INGTON] MAY 18TH 1874.[110]

REV. E. D NEILL (NOW PREST OF —— COLLEGE NEAR ST. Paul Minn.) was on duty as a Clerk at the White House from —— [1864] to —— [1865]. Passing the door of Prest Lincolns office, on the morning after the second election, and seeing the door partially open he entered, and drawing up a chair near L. congratulated him upon his re-election. The Prest received him kindly, and throwing up his spectacles, chatted familiarly with him for some minutes. Mr. Neill does not re-member the details of the conversation; but what particularly struck him, was that the bundle of papers which the Prest. had been intently poring over was the record of a Court-Martial trial of a private soldier condemned to be shot, whose sentence had been suspended; and Mr. Neill concluded that a man who could go back to his office and resolutely take up the dull routine drudgery of his post with such equanimity, on the morning after a triumphant reelection to the Presidency under the peculiar and exciting circumstances then existing, must be a man full of the elements of greatness, and one who would not lose his self-posses-sion on any probable emergency.

CONVERSATION WITH VICE PRESIDENT WILSON NOV. 16 1875[111]

CALLED TO SEE THE VICE PRESIDENT AT THE REQUEST OF Judge Davis to ask after his convalescence—found him in bed, not so well as yesterday but nevertheless getting along encouragingly.

He asked after the progress of our book and in talking with him about it he said

"Wade, who as you know was on the Committee on the Conduct of the War was talking to Lincoln one day, berating McClellan, and urging that the command be taken from him.

"Well, Wade, said the President, now put yourself for a moment in my place. If I relieve McClellan, whom shall I put in command? Who of all these men is to supersede him?

"Why, said Wade, anybody

Wade, replied Lincoln, "*anybody*" will do for you, but not for me. I must have *somebody*.

SUMNER
VICE PREST. WILSON IN CONVERSATION WITH J G. N IN HIS OFFICE AT WASHINGTON APL 1ST 1874.[112]

Y OU KNOW THAT A GREAT MANY SENATORS WERE OPPOSED TO Lincoln, even after his second nomination. My colleague (Sumner) was among them. Why he said to me at one time in the Senate that he (Lincoln) was utterly unfit to be President. "Why" said he "there are twenty men in the Senate who are better qualified for the place."

"Well Sumner," I asked, "who are they?"

"Why you" replied Sumner, "and Judge Collamer (turning to him) and A & B & C" naming others &c.

CHIEF JUSTICE CHASE
J. G. N. CONVERSATION WITH V P WILSON IN MY OFFICE AT WASHINGTON THIS 1ST APRIL 1874[113]

W ILSON SAYS HE WAS ON HIS WAY FROM THE TREASURY TO the War Department, when he was met by Blair. Blair stopped him and said "Wilson I am a candidate for C[*hief*] J[*ustice*] and I should like to have you for me."

"But I am for Chase" replied Wilson.

"Well" rejoined Blair, "Chase will not be nominated. It will almost certainly be one of those old fogies on the Supreme bench and I am sure you would prefer me to them."

Wilson replied that he was a Chase man and must continue in his support to the end. A little startled however by the very confident tone in which Blair disposed of Chase's prospects, instead of going on to the War Department for which he had started, he turned in at the White house and at once sought the President whom he happened to find alone.

"I came to talk with you about Chase Mr. Presdt" said he; "I hope you will appoint him first because it would greatly gratify the anti-slavery men, for Chase very clearly defined this contest as early as '41; but more especially, because the Supreme Court is going to have very great power over a variety of questions which will of necessity grow out of the war, and with Chase on the bench we should be entirely safe. I know that Chase said many very harsh things about you during the summer, and of which you have probably heard. But they did you no harm, and in view of all the circumstances you can afford to overlook them."

"Oh, as to that," replied Lincoln, "I don't care for all that. That will make no difference whatever in my action. Of Chase's ability and of his soundness on the general issues of the war there is of course no question. I have only had one doubt about his appointment. He is a man of unbounded ambition, and has been working all his life to become President; that he can never be; and I fear that if I make him Chief Justice, he will simply become more restless and uneasy, and neglect the place in his strife and intrigue to make himself President. He has got the Presidential maggot in his head and it will wriggle there as long as it is warm. If I were sure that he would go upon the bench and give up his aspirations to do anything but make himself a great judge, I would send in his name at once."[114]

3

Other Interviews and Two Essays by Nicolay

[*CONVERSATION WITH NATHANIEL P. BANKS,*
SEPTEMBER 1887][1]

IN A CONVERSATION I HAD WITH GENL BANKS IN SEPT. 1887 I asked him whether there was any truth in the rumor mysteriously whispered about in certain quarters that Pres. Lincoln had ordered the Red River expedition against the judgment of Genl Banks merely to accommodate certain cotton speculators; that these had brought an autograph letter from the Pres. to the Genl. of a confidential nature conveying the request in such terms that the Genl. neither felt at liberty to disregard it nor to make it public.

Genl. Banks emphatically denied the truth of this story. He said the fact was that he was opposed to the Red River expedition. That he had written Genl. Halleck at least twenty dispatches informing him that he opposed it. That he (Banks) thought the movement against Texas, which as he gathered was desired more for diplomatic than military reasons ought to be made by way of Galveston and the coast where little rebel opposition would have been encountered; but that Halleck seemed to be bent on the movement up Red River and peremptorily ordered it against his (Banks's) judgment and advice.

The Genl. also said that Admiral Porter also gave all his influence in favor of the Red River movement, although when it was determined upon he was so slow in preparing for it as to practically have caused its failure.[2] By the time Porter got his gunboats ready the water was so low in Red River as to greatly increase the extent of loss and disaster. Genl. Banks also strongly hinted that Porter was much more interested in securing cotton to [be] adjudicated by a naval prize court which he was running than about the military success of the expedition.

As to the cotton speculators he said they did bring him a letter from the Pres. but that it distinctly directed him (Banks) not to allow their operations in any wise to interfere with or to hazard military success. That these speculators did on their own responsibility go out in advance of the army and gather up cotton, but that when they brought it within the lines he (Banks) seized it for military uses and actually did use it, putting it into the dam which his engineers built to float the gunboats over the shallows in the retreat, and by that means saved them.

STATEMENT BY DR. PARKER[3]

DR PARKER STATES THAT HE WAS PRESENT WHEN A DELEGA-tion of ministers called on Prest L—after usual address on such occasions—he came forward with head bowed down and replied—

"I may not be a great man—(straightening up to his full height) I *know* I am not a great man—and perhaps it is better that it is so—for it makes me rely upon One who is great and who has the wisdom and power to lead us safely through this great trial &c.

CONVERSATION WITH HON. F. W. SEWARD
JANY 9TH 1879[4]

AT THE TIME OF THE SENATORIAL CABINET CRISIS [*IN December 1862*]—[*Ira*] Harris came in to the State Department on Saturday ? morning, rubbing his hands and smiling. "Well, said he, that affair is coming out all right. I have just had a talk with the President who told me he had received the resignation of Mr. Chase. 'Now,' said Lincoln, 'I can ride: I have a pumpkin in each end of my bag.' "[5]

STATEMENT BY A SON OF MR. CRISFIELD
OF MARYLAND[6]

THE PEACE CONVENTION WAS IN SESSION IN WASHINGTON when Mr Lincoln reached the capital a few days before his inauguration, and by formal resolution the members proceeded in a body to call on the President-Elect.[7] One of their number, Mr Crisfield of Md. often told the story that it was his lot to walk with Hon. Wm. C. Rives of Va., a man of very short stature and generally insignificant presence.[8] When Mr Crisfield introduced him, Mr Lincoln said humorously,

"Why, I had supposed that all Virginia statesmen were great men!"

Mr Rives however both failed to appreciate the joke or to respond to it. He replied with a very solemn face and a stiff formal bow "Sir, I feel very humble in this presence."

[ROBERT TODD LINCOLN'S REMINISCENCES, GIVEN 5 JANUARY 1885][9]

IN JULY 1863, WHILE I WAS IN WASHINGTON DURING THE VA-cation of Harvard College, and after the battle of Gettysburgh, I went into my father's office room at the time in the afternoon at which he was accustomed to leave his office to go to the Soldiers Home, and found him in [much] distress, his head leaning upon the desk in front of him, and when he raised his head there were evidences of tears upon his face. Upon my asking the cause of his distress he told me that he had just received the information that Gen. Lee had succeeded in escaping across the Potomac river at Williamsport without serious molestation by Gen. Meade's army. He then told me that after the battle of Gettysburgh and after Lee reached the Potomac River and after our army had closed in upon him at that point, he felt sure that the final blow could be struck, and he summoned Gen. Haupt, in whom he had great confidence as a bridge builder, and asked him how long in view of the materials which might be supposed to be available under Lee, would it take him to devise the means and get his army across the river.[10] That Gen. Haupt after re-flection replied that if he were Gen. Lee's chief engineer, he could devise the means and put him across the river with the materials at hand within twenty four hours, and he had no doubt that Gen. Lee had just as good engineers for that purpose as he was. My father then said that he at once sent an order to Gen. Meade (I do not recollect that he told me whether the order was telegraphic or by messenger) directing him to attack Lee's army with all his force immediately, and that if he was successful in the attack he might destroy the order, but if he was unsuccessful he might preserve it for his vindication. My father then told me that instead of attacking upon the receipt of the order, a council of war had been held, as he understood, with the result that no attack was made, and Lee got across the river without serious molestation.

[MEMORANDUM BY ROBERT TODD LINCOLN, EVIDENTLY WRITTEN FOR NICOLAY, 2 JANUARY 1885][11]

ON ONE OF MY VISITS TO WASHINGTON, THE EXACT DATE OF which I do not recollect, as I was passing from the private part of the house up to Mr Nicolay's or Mr Hay's office, I found a considerable crowd in the corridor, of persons anxious to see the President; and one of them, Simon Hanscomb,[12] came to me as I was passing, and said that he was very anxious to see the President, that it was very urgent that he should do so, and he showed me a printed circular as I recollect, perhaps the one afterwards called to "Pomeroy circular"[13]. . . . Possibly I said to the doorkeeper that I would be glad to have him let Mr Hanscomb in as soon as he could. In the evening after dinner as I was in my private room in the house, my father strolled in and showed me a letter from Mr Chase, then Secretary of the Treasury, which as I recall was a brief note saying in substance that after what has occurred to day he deemed it proper to tender his resignation, &c. My father asked me to lay out writing materials for him, and at my table he wrote a short note to Mr Chase in which he said in substance "that he knew of no reason why he should not remain in the Cabinet."[14] Upon his showing this note to me I expressed surprise, at that part of the note here specified and asked him if he had not seen the circular. He stopped me and said he didn't know any thing about it; that a good many people during the day had tried to see him and tell him something which he supposed was some new sign of Chase's deviltry, and it did not suit him to know any thing about it, and that therefore the remark in his letter declining to accept his resignation was strictly true. Thereupon at his request I called a messenger, and the note to Mr Chase was sent.[15]

TOLD BY J G N[ICOLAY][16]

SEC CHASE CAME UP TO THE WHITE HOUSE ONE DAY TO SEE the President, and said Mr P[resident] I dont see how we can stand this great expenditure, 2 or 3 Millions a day, it is dreadful, what shall be done. After thinking a moment Mr Lincoln said, well Mr Sec I dont know, unless you give your paper mill another turn. Chase was disgusted at the levity[17]

[CONVERSATION WITH WILLIAM M. SPRINGER, 31 JANUARY 1887][18]

TALKING TODAY WITH THE HON. WM M SPRINGER OF ILLINOIS (January 31 1887) he told me that he was present at Fords Theatre on the night of Lincoln's assassination, sitting six or eight rows back from the stage. That when Booth jumped or fell from the stage-box there was perfect silence and quiet in the whole house until Booth raised himself from his fall and flourishing his knife in his hand walked deliberately and unmolested diagonally across the stage. About the moment he disappeared behind the wings there was a shriek from Mrs Lincoln in the box, which seemed to break the spell of stupefaction which had fallen upon the house. Thereupon the audience rose almost *en masse* and several persons sprang forward and climbed upon the stage, himself being one of the first of these. He called for a doctor in the audience and several coming forward he assisted one of them to climb up into the President's box.

Mr Springer says Stuarts testimony about chasing Booth across the stage has not a particle of foundation in fact.[19]

M R. LINCOLN'S NOMINATION FOR PRESIDENT OF COURSE
made it necessary that he should give up all attention to private
business. The building at that time serving as the State Capitol stood in
the public square at Springfield, a plain but dignified structure of brown-
ish stone, containing the usual legislative halls and during the early history of the State ample accommodations for the business of its executive
administration; though in latter times it has been superseded by a much
larger building in another part of the city. The governor's room in the
old State House not being needed except when the Legislature was in
session, was set apart for Mr. Lincoln's use as a reception room. There the
public had free access to the new candidate, a privilege of which both the
local citizens and numerous visitors from a distance freely availed themselves. To this room Mr. Lincoln usually came in the morning between
nine and ten, bringing with him the letters he had received during the
night at his own home, and about which he gave such directions to his
private secretary (the writer) as they severally required. Most of them
needed no answer, being simply messages of congratulation. Those from
intimate personal friends he usually acknowledged with his own hand;
and these indicate from the first a considerable confidence that he would
be elected—a confidence inspired by political signs which his own experience and sagacity enabled him correctly to interpret.[21]

For two classes of letters which came in considerable numbers, Mr.
Lincoln prepared the following specific formulas with which his private
secretary might reply:

(Biography)

Springfield, Illinois, _____ 1860

Dear Sir: Your letter to Mr. Lincoln of _____ and by
which you seek his assistance in getting up a biographical

sketch of him, is received. Applications of this class are so numerous that it is simply impossible for him to attend to them.

Yours &c.

J. G. Nicolay.

(Doctrine)

Springfield, Illinois, _____ 1860

Dear Sir: Your letter to Mr. Lincoln of _____ and by which you seek to obtain his opinions on certain political points, has been received by him. He has received others of a similar character; but he also has a greater number of the exactly opposite character. The latter beseech him to write nothing whatever upon any point of political doctrine. They say his positions were well known when he was nominated, and that he must not now embarrass the canvass by undertaking to shift or modify them. He regrets that he cannot oblige all, but you perceive it is impossible for him to do so.

Yours &c.

J. G. Nicolay

Of course a few exceptions were made, for special reasons, in each of these classes of replies. Biographies of some character were sure to appear, and it was better that they should be correct than incorrect. An application of this kind came from influential personal friends in Columbus, Ohio, in behalf of a young writer whose name had at that time been little heard in the literary world; and for his use Mr. Lincoln wrote with his own hand a short autobiographical sketch covering the equivalent of about thirteen or fourteen pages of foolscap. From a copy of this manuscript William D. Howells wrote a "Life of Abraham Lincoln" of 78 small octavo pages which has long since been forgotten, because the mighty events of the War of the Rebellion lifted the subject, and the irrepressible force of genius raised the author to a fame that eclipses the beginnings of both their careers.[22]

Mr. Lincoln of course watched the progress of the campaign with great solicitude, but his personal action in it was of the very slightest. No "literary bureau" or other electioneering organization to influence the country at large existed at Springfield; the headquarters of the National Committee being as usual at New York. The few letters which Mr. Lincoln wrote on the subject, and they probably did not exceed half a dozen, were letters of inquiry as to the situation at given times rather than of direction or even suggestion as to what should be done.

About the middle of July, and while the presidential campaign seemed to be progressing in a way reasonably satisfactory to Republicans, Mr. Lincoln received intimations that Hon. Richard W. Thompson of Terre Haute Indiana (afterwards Secretary of the Navy under President Hayes) very much desired a private interview with him.[23] Mr. Lincoln was well acquainted with Mr. Thompson; he knew him to be an astute politician who had formerly been an ardent Whig, but since the dissolution of that party had become affiliated with the "Know Nothings" or "Americans," and now represented perhaps more than any other western man, what remained of the strength and vitality of that faction, which, though no longer an influential third party, as in the preceding presidential election, was yet supposed to possess an important minority effectiveness that might control the result in a few States.[24] While it was important to secure these little balances of power for the Republican ticket, there was on the other hand danger that too open an alliance might drive off an equal or greater number of foreign voters to whom the "Know Nothing" principles and objects were exceedingly obnoxious. The greatest caution was therefore necessary, for Democratic newspapers had been industriously charging Mr. Lincoln, not only with "Know Nothing" tendencies, but with being actually a member of a "Know Nothing" lodge—a charge however which he explicitly denied in a confidential letter to a friend.[25]

Mr. Lincoln therefore, instead of inviting Mr. Thompson to Springfield, sent the writer to hold an interview with him at Terre Haute, giving him the following brief written instructions for his guidance:

Ascertain what he wants.
On what subject he would confer with me.

And the particulars, if he will give them.
Is an interview indispensable?
And if so, how soon must it be had?
Tell him my motto is "Fairness to all."
But commit me to nothing.

It is only this scrap of writing which makes the incident at all worthy of record. There could be no better exemplification of Mr. Lincoln's character and caution than this short memorandum of instructions. It reflects all his directness of method, all his sincerity of dealing, all his determination to keep free from any entanglements of intrigue, and to expressly avoid any inferential obligations. "Commit me to nothing" is his positive injunction; on the other hand the announcement of his motto "Fairness to all" is the promise of that broad liberality which he carried out as President, and through which he maintained the easy party leadership that secured his renomination and re-election.[26]

These two items of instruction find a curious parallel in his later career. When, in the following December, after his triumphant election, he sent Seward his letter tendering him the office of Secretary of State, it repeated his motto of "Fairness to all" in this significant sentence: "In regard to the patronage sought with so much eagerness and jealousy, I have prescribed for myself the maxim 'Fairness to all;' and I earnestly beseech your cooperation in keeping the maxim good." So also, when about four years later he sent Mr. Seward to meet the rebel commissioners at the Hampton Roads Conference to talk over possible negotiations for peace, the letter of instruction he gave him (before he determined to go personally) contained these important and unmistakable qualifications of his mission: "You will hear all they may choose to say, and report it to me. You will not assume to definitely consummate anything." It is the discerning spirit and guiding hand of a great master, alike in party politics and national statesmanship.

It only remains to add that in the interview which the writer held with Mr. Thompson the latter gentleman sought only to be assured of the general "fairness" to all elements giving Mr Lincoln their support, and that he did not even hint at any exaction or promise as being necessary to secure the "Know Nothing" vote for the Republican ticket; and this unbought good will no doubt contributed its share to the handsome majorities which Mr. Lincoln received in all the Western States.[27]

It was one of the important characteristics of the campaign of 1860 that it enlisted to an unusual degree the interest and efforts of the clergymen of all denominations in the United States. The religious aspect of the slavery question had been as zealously discussed—perhaps more zealously even than its economical or political aspects. For six years Douglas had boldly challenged and denied the right of clergymen to "preach politics"; and clergymen had as courageously defended their right to discuss all moral issues whether involved in politics or not. Therefore when Lincoln was nominated, preachers desired especially to know what kind of man he was, and it may be interesting to read the following extracts of letters written by Rev. Albert Hale, Pastor of the Second Presbyterian Church of Springfield[28] to Rev. Theron Baldwin of New Jersey, describing Mr. Lincoln during the campaign.

Springfield, May 31, 1860.

Dear Brother Baldwin:
    Yours of the 24th came in due time, and I embrace a few moments to reply. Mr. Lincoln is not an attendant on my preaching. His wife is a member of the First Presbyterian Church, and when he is in the city he pretty regularly attends there on the Sabbath. It has been whispered of late that he does not attend so frequently because the pastor is afflicted with Douglas proclivities. I do not credit this report for the reason that Mr. Lincoln is not in the habit of showing his resentment every time an opportunity offers. If of late he is more frequently absent on the Sabbath it is undoubtedly to be accounted for by the fact that for the last three or four years he has been away from home much of the time and engaged in very exhausting labors. He may be regarded as a regular attendant on the preaching of the Gospel, but with western and not puritan views of the method of Sabbath observance.

He once taught a class in Sabbath School but not in this place. I always presume he is a believer in the divine origin of the Christian religion and not a skeptic. From the frequency and readiness with which he is accustomed to quote from the Bible and the use he makes of such quotations it is clear that he has read and pondered its contents.[29] I wish I could say that he is born of God.

His moral character stands among us here without reproach or blemish. I have known him for twenty years, and latterly as circumstances have made him more prominent I have become well acquainted with him, and have watched the course of public opinion in these parts, both among his friends and his foes. My residence here at the Capital where the streams of political corruption from all parts of the State and the land meet, has made me sufficiently distrustful of the integrity and virtue of public men. If not "all men," at least all public men have seemed to be "liars."

Abraham Lincoln has been here all the time, consulting and consulted by all classes, all parties, and on all subjects of political interest, with men of every degree of influence and every degree of corruption and yet I have never heard even an enemy accuse him of intentional dishonesty or corruption. When the crisis was approaching at Chicago[30] earnestly was he beset by interested friends to allow them to "negotiate" if necessary to secure his nomination and his reply you may read in the little scrap which I enclose, and which is true as I ascertain by inquiry. As he sat today in his office with men calling on him from all quarters deeply interested in his election he was heard to say: "Gentlemen, I am not elected President of the United States and have made no pledges to any man and intend to make none." He has stood before the community here the man of uncorrupted if not incorruptible integrity, and to be able to say that of any man who has mingled as freely with Illinois politics and politicians as Mr. Lincoln has is glory enough for one man.[31]

Springfield, Illinois, June 15, 1860.

Dear Brother Baldwin:

Yours came last night. If anything I have written can be made useful in the present campaign, in behalf of Mr. Lincoln I most cheerfully take off "the hoops" and allow it to flow out. If I recollect rightly, I mentioned that Mr. Lincoln had said to all that he had made no pledges and if elected to the office of President of the United States he should go to the White House without a pledge to any man or party. In other words that he would not buy the votes of the people and pay with pledges of official favor and patronage. I said this, if at all, on the authority of good men and true, who assured me that they understood it and were authorized to say so. Knowing that this is not the modern way of making the more important office holders, especially the President, I have taken the liberty to call on him and inquire. About one hour ago I sat with him in his room, and made inquiry as above. His reply was in substance: That he had made no pledge of office, honor, or patronage in any way, to any man or party, on the condition of his election to the Presidency, and he was most happy to say that very little of the kind had been sought, and that, so unimportant as to draw from him no reply. "For instance," said he, "some few rather silly persons have by letter applied, saying, that in case of my election they would like the appointment of Postmaster in their place—all of them very unimportant places and I have not replied to one of them." And he added: "I have made no pledges, and the Lord helping me I shall make none. I shall go to Washington, if at all, an unpledged man." As I rose to go, and gave him my hand, he held on and said: "Mr. Hale, I have read my Bible some, though not half as much as I ought, and I have always regarded Peter as sincere when he said he would never deny his Master. Yet he did deny Him. Now I think I shall keep my word, and maintain the stand I have taken—but then I must remember that I am liable to infirmity and may fall." We still held each other warmly by the hand while I replied: "And may He who kept Peter in the right way after the terrible experiences of his fall, keep you firm and faithful without any such experience," and so we parted. In the course of our interview and in reference to this subject I said to him, that it was a new way of making a President, but a right way, and that it was time for a stern rebuke to be administered to the cherished expectations of party men whose only qualification for office was their ability to make a noise, and their keen appetite for spoils—all of which he affirmed in his calm and earnest way.[32]

Springfield, November 13, 1860.

Dear Brother Baldwin:

. . . Mr. Lincoln is entirely calm. I was with him in his room an hour yesterday. He was interested just then in the returns (so far as received) from Missouri. The State has probably gone for Bell, though the returns up to this time show a small majority for Douglas.[33] There is a stream of visitors at Mr. Lincoln's room—from all parts and for all conceivable reasons. While I was with him an elderly and very good-looking lady came in to take the hand of the coming President, and to remind him that twenty three years ago he ate a meal at her house, and when she apologized for not having a better dinner for him, he replied: "Madam, it is good enough for the President." Just as she was telling her story two tall sandy-haired young men entered who were strangers. As soon as the old lady had finished her story, one of them came toward Mr. Lincoln and said: "Mr. Lincoln, how tall are you?" "Six feet, four inches," was his reply. "Well," said the sucker, "they say I am just as tall as you." "Just stand up beside this wall," said Mr. Lincoln. He did so and then Mr. Lincoln stood in the same place, and proved to be of the same height exactly. I give these only as specimens of the singular and often trifling things, which occur at his room daily. There is a constant stream coming and going, from every part of the land. One day several weeks ago two country boys came along the dark passage that leads to his room. One of them looked in at the door, and then called to his fellow behind saying: "Come on, he is here." The boys entered and he spoke to them and immediately one of them said that it was reported in their neighborhood that he (Mr. Lincoln) had been poisoned, and their father had sent them to see if the report was true. "And," says the boy with all earnestness, "Dad says you must look out, and eat nothing only what your old woman cooks, and mother says so too," and the lads took their leave.[34]

The pride which his old-time friends and neighbors felt in the rare good fortune that one of their own class had become a real presidential candidate and might become a real President of the United States—an elevation none the less impressive because they had heard it so often vaunted as the privilege and possibility of every American school-boy, is further exemplified in the letter he received from one of his intimate comrades in the Black Hawk War:

May 29, 1860

Respected Sir:

In view of the intimacy that at one time subsisted between yourself and me, I deem it to be my duty as well as privilege, now that the intensity of the excitement of recent transactions is a little passed from you and from me, after the crowd of congratulations already received from many friends, also to offer you my heartfelt congratulations on your very exalted position in our great Republican party. No doubt but that you will become tired of the flattery of cringing, selfish

adulators. But I think you will know that way [*what*] I say I
feel. For the attachment commenced in the Black Hawk campaign while we messed together with Johnson, Fancher, and
Wyatt, when we ground our coffee in the same tin cup with
the hatchet handle—baked our bread on our ramrods around
the same fire—ate our fried meat off the same piece of elm
bark—slept in the same tent every night—traveled together
by day and by night in search of the savage foe—and together
scoured the tall grass on the battle ground of the skirmish
near Gratiot's Grove in search of the slain—with very many
incidents too tedious to name—and consummated on our
afoot and canoe journey home, must render us incapable of
deception.[35] Since the time mentioned, our pursuits have
called me to operate a little apart; yours, as you formerly
hinted, to a course of political and legal struggle; mine to
agriculture and medicine. The success that we have both
enjoyed, I am happy to know, is very encouraging. I am
also glad to know, although we must act in vastly different
spheres, that we are enlisted for the promotion of the same
great cause: the cause which, next to revealed religion (which
is humility and love) is most dear: the cause of Liberty, as set
forth by true republicanism and not rank abolitionism.

Then let us go on in the discharge of duty, trusting, for
aid, to the Great Universal Ruler.

Yours truly,
George M. Harrison

In the first months of the campaign all four parties in the field were
too much occupied in eulogizing their candidates and perfecting their
electioneering organizations to allow disunion feelings and disunion
threats to manifest themselves to any note-worthy degree; and one of
Mr. Lincoln's letters shows us that as yet he entertained no serious apprehension that the extreme fire-eaters of the South would be able to

draw the people of their States into a formidable revolutionary movement:

Springfield, Illinois August 15, 1860.

My dear Sir:

Yours of the 9th inclosing the letter of Hon. John Minor Botts was duly received.[36] The letter is herewith returned according to your request. It contains one of the many assurances I receive from the South, that in no probable event will there be any very formidable effort to break up the Union. The people of the South have too much of good sense and good temper to attempt the ruin of the government rather than see it administered by the men who made it. At least so I hope and believe. I thank you both for your letter and a sight of that of Mr. Botts.

Yours very truly,
A. Lincoln

John B. Fry Esq.[37]

His optimism was doubtless inspired not alone by such letters as Mr. Botts had written, but more particularly by what he personally knew of the character and feeling of the people of his native State of Kentucky, which knowledge was strongly supported by information coming to him during the campaign, of which the following letter from an influential Kentucky politician who had taken a prominent part in the Baltimore Convention which nominated Bell and Everett is a fair example:[38]

Lexington, Kentucky, May 22, 1860.

Dear Sir:

You and your wife both being Kentuckians by birth, I congratulate the country and both of you on your nomination at

Chicago. I have no fears of an old Clay Whig forgetting his native land and blood, and risking the Union by running after religious or political theories and abstractions.

The case would have been very different if Mr. Seward had been chosen. With your election—if a patriotic, moderate, and liberal policy is pursued, such as General Jackson recommended to Mr. Monroe, the conservative Slave States will be satisfied and help to take care of the volcanic South. So far as I may take a part in the canvass, I shall do you justice—full justice. . . .

Very Respectfully your most obedient servant,

Leslie Coombs

The great variety of opinions, advice, and suggestions which were contained in the correspondence addressed to him may also be inferred from the draft of an answer which he sketched, apparently for the mere purpose of giving vent to the humor they excited in him—for the letter seems never to have been finished or sent:

Springfield, Illinois, August 27, 1860.

C. H. Fisher

Dear Sir:

Your second note inclosing the supposed speech of Mr. Dallas to Lord Brougham is received. I have read the speech quite through, together with the real author's introductory and closing remarks. I have also looked through the long preface of the book today.[39] Both seem to be well written and contain many things with which I could agree, and some with which I could not. A specimen of the latter is the declaration in the closing remarks upon the "speech," that the institution [*of slavery*] is a "necessity" imposed on us by the negro race. That the going many thousand miles, seizing a set of savages, bringing them here, and making slaves of them is a necessity imposed on us by them involves a species of logic to which my mind will scarcely assent.

The enforced idleness to which Mr. Lincoln's candidacy compelled him during the long summer from his nomination on the 18th of May until his election on the 6th of November, must have seemed a strange contrast to him as compared with his constant activity in previous presidential and other campaigns. In the Fremont campaign four years before, he had made over fifty speeches; in the senatorial campaign two years before, he had made probably a hundred. Now his whole time was given to the quiet reception of visitors at his room in the State House, where, indeed, they came in considerable numbers, leaving little time for anything except the exchange of greetings and mere desultory talk, in which his whole effort was necessarily directed to avoiding political subjects, since any expression of opinion would be instantly telegraphed and printed far and wide. In this however he was very successful. He was by nature genial and social, a ready and entertaining talker, able to invest the tritest topics with fresh interest by his comments which were always clear and forcible, and often quaint and original. The visits from his old friends and neighbors from Sangamon County and the reminiscences of frontier days furnished a considerable share of such conversation. The popular enthusiasm had seized with eagerness upon the incidents of his early life as pioneer and rail-splitter. His room became a perfect museum of symbolic presents in the form of axes, mauls, wedges, log-chains, and other paraphanalia of the woodman's craft, and afforded him the opportunity to entertain ever his polished city-bred callers with explanations and anecdotes about the use or importance of these, to them, unfamiliar implements, by help of which the men of the backwoods subdued the wilderness.

In one quality of greatness which Scripture defines as he that ruleth his spirit is better than he that taketh a city, Mr. Lincoln was preeminent; his self control was simply wonderful. During more than four years the writer had opportunities almost daily and nightly to witness his bearing under most trying conditions and circumstances, and during the whole time never saw him manifest any extraordinary excitement beyond that of an eager interest to acquire information, or indulge in any violence of speech or action beyond that of impressive emphasis, either in comment or command; while on the other hand he was never phlegmatic or indifferent even when annoyed by the most trivial requests, or patiently enduring the waste of precious time by the most wearisome of bores.

This equipoise of manner, this patience of spirit, this calmness of judgment, which were destined not to be fully tried till after his inauguration as President, would have easily carried him through the anxieties of the presidential canvass even had its results hung more in doubt. But the prospects of Republican success from the very beginning grew brighter and brighter. The second disruption of the Democratic party at Baltimore; the constantly growing antagonism between the Douglas and Buchanan factions; the auspicious result of the Maine election in September; the practical failure of a few time-serving leaders in the three opposing parties to effect "fusion" in a few doubtful States upon the basis of a division of the spoils; and finally the triumphant Republican victories in the October elections, followed each other in an accelerating political drift. Even before the last mentioned event he was able to foresee his own probable election, as shown by his letter to his friend Dr. Henry in Oregon:[40]

Springfield, Illinois, September 22, 1860.

Dear Doctor:

Yours of July 18th was received some time ago. When you wrote you had not heard the result of the Democratic convention at Charleston and Baltimore. With the two tickets in the field I should think it possible for our friends to carry Oregon. But the general result, I think, does not depend upon Oregon. No one this side of the mountains pretends that any ticket can be elected by the people, unless it be ours. Hence great efforts to combine against us are being made, which, however, as yet have not had much success. Besides what we see in the newspapers, I have a good deal of private correspondence; and without giving details, I will only say it all looks very favorable to our success.

Your friend as ever,
A. Lincoln

The culmination of the campaign in so far as it was connected with Mr. Lincoln's personal deportment, cannot perhaps be better described than by quoting the following extract from a newspaper report about election day at Springfield; an event, which though it brought out the usual party zeal of western towns was nevertheless in all respects entirely quiet and orderly:

Since every Republican vote in the county was needed, as likely to affect the result in the State Legislature, Mr. Lincoln had determined not to withhold his, but had intended to wait until toward evening, before going to the polls, in order to avoid, as much as possible, encountering a crowd. At about three o'clock however, he was informed that the way was as clear as it probably would be at any time, and he decided to go over at once. . . . On his way across to the Court House Mr. Lincoln was not unobserved; but as soon as he stood upon the sidewalk, and advanced to the steps, he was recognized and welcomed with such a cheer as no man ever received who has not the hearts as well as the voices of his people. Every vestige of party feeling seemed to be suddenly abandoned. Even the distributors of the Douglas tickets shouted and swung their hats as wildly as the rest. Mr. Lincoln walked leisurely through the hall and up the stairway, followed by as many of the multitude as could get near him, and, on entering the voting room, was hailed with a burst of enthusiasm which almost extinguished the remembrance of that which he had just received below. Then, too, there was no sign of political feeling. I saw a spry old party, with his hands full of Democratic documents forget his special function so far as to prance upon a railing, and to take the lead in an infinite series of Lincoln cheers. The object of all this irrepressible delight took it as calmly as he could, and, urging his way to the voting table, deposited the straight Republican ticket. After thus serving his friends, he turned toward the door again and endeavored to pass out. It would have seemed impossible for greater enthusiasm to be now shown than was before displayed, but the crowd certainly tried their best at it. Then Mr. Lincoln took off his hat, and smiled all around upon them; and when he smiles heartily there is something in it good to see. So his neighbors thought, too, for a number came about him to shake him by the hand and have a few words with him as he moved along. But this was soon over, and he was suffered to return to his more quiet quarters at the State House, from which—so quickly it had all passed—he had not probably been absent more than five minutes.[41]

At about nine o'clock on the night of that eventful day, the Republicans of Springfield filled the Representatives' Hall of the State House to overflowing to await and hear the election returns that were beginning to come from the State and Nation. On one side of the public square in which the State House stood were gathered in a large second story room over one of the principal stores two or three score of the wives and daughters of prominent Republicans, leaders of Springfield society, decorating the room with flags, and spreading a bountiful improvised collation—quite as eager as the most excited street politician in the State House to learn whether presidential honors had certainly fallen upon the city. At the same hour, on another side of the public square, in a small second story room occupied by the Western Union Telegraph, sat Mr. Lincoln alone, excepting only the superintendent and operators, where undisturbed by any sound save that of the clicking instruments and the ever increasing volume of distant hurrahs that floated across the street from the State House, he read the telegrams that were silently handed him, conveying from every northern State decisive news of the great political change which the day had wrought.

"SOME INCIDENTS IN LINCOLN'S JOURNEY FROM SPRINGFIELD TO WASHINGTON"[42]

THE WRITER DOES NOT KNOW AT WHAT TIME MR. LINCOLN began the composition of his Inaugural Address. While it is probable that he did not set himself seriously at this task until after the result of the November election had been ascertained beyond doubt, it is quite possible that not only had the subject been considered with great deliberation during the summer, but that sentences or propositions, and perhaps paragraphs of it had been put in writing; for Mr. Lincoln often resorted to the process of cumulative thought, and his constant tendency to, and great success in axiomatic definition, resulted in a large measure from a habit he had acquired of reducing a forcible idea or an epigrammatic sentence or phrase to writing, and keeping it until further reasoning enabled him to add other sentences or additional phrases to complete or supplement the first—to elaborate or to conclude his point or argument. There were many of these scraps among his papers, seldom in the shape of mere rough notes, but almost always in the form of a finished proposition or statement—a habit showing great prudence and deliberation of thought, and evincing a corresponding strength and solidity of opinion and argument.

It was of course necessary to preserve the utmost secrecy in the preparation and transcription of the Inaugural. Springfield was full of both politicians and newspaper reporters who would have left no stone unturned to see even a scrap of his writing about the public questions of that day. Neither his own house nor the office where he received his numerous daily visitors could be used for this work. But a retreat was found for him completely safe from prying inquisition. His brother-in-law had a large store on the public square in Springfield, in the second story of which a small counting room had been partitioned off, which at the time was not in use.[43] There he could hide himself, and the way to it easily foiled inquiring pursuit, and there the Inaugural was written and copied, and nearly every surplus fragment of manuscript destroyed. Fortunately

107

for us, one such fragment—the first draft of the first sentence, of the first Inaugural was preserved, and is here given in *facsimile*.

When it was finished the manuscript was intrusted to the publisher of the Illinois State Journal, who taking a trusty compositor and a case of type, locked himself in a room of the Journal office, and remained there until the document was set up, the necessary proofs taken, and the form secure in the office safe until Mr. Lincoln could correct and revise the proofs.[44] A second and a third revision necessitated slight changes after which an edition of about a dozen copies was printed, and the type distributed—all under the eyes of the publisher. Perfect secrecy was maintained, perfect faith was kept. Only the persons authorized knew that the work was done.[45]

Though the Inaugural had then been successfully written and printed it was yet destined to run serious danger of coming to premature publicity. It will be remembered that Mr. Lincoln was carried from Springfield to Washington in a special train, accompanied by his family and a small suite of friends; but also that his journey comprised a visit, by official invitation of Governors and Legislatures, to the Capitals of all the States which lay in or near his route of travel. To carry the precious document over this long distance, through all the delay, hurly-burly, and confusion incident to such a trip was no easy problem. The President-elect therefore placed it together with other papers in a small, old-fashioned black oilcloth carpetbag, and on the morning of starting from Springfield gave it into the hands of his son Robert—late minister to England—with general injunctions to see to its safety, but not informing him that it contained the Inaugural. Robert was a school boy, not yet eighteen years old, full of the exuberance and carelessness peculiar to that age, to whom this trip seemed more of a triumphal journey than to his serious father; for in the recent Presidential Campaign by way of a pendant to Lincoln's sobriquet of "Illinois Rail-Splitter" the irrepressible newspaper humor of the country had facetiously dubbed Robert "The Prince of Rails;" and at almost every stopping place a little clan of "The Boys" of his own age was ready to seize upon him and do him the honors after their own capricious whims. The first stopping place was Indianapolis, and the following quotation is from the newspaper report of the arrival:

At five oclock the train stopped at the crossing of Washington Street where it was met by members of the Legislature, the officers of State, the City Council, the Military Companies of the city, the Fire Department of Indianapolis, and thousands of men, women, and children, on foot, in carriages, and on horseback. . . . [After describing the formation of the official procession, the report continues.][46] Remarking here, parenthetically, we regret to say that most of the carriages prepared for Mr. Lincoln's suite and the committee of arrangements, were taken possession of by outsiders, compelling many of those who came from Springfield with Mr. Lincoln, including his son (the "Prince of Rails,") and some of his intimate and personal friends, to walk to the Bates House with their carpetsacks in hand and force their way through the dense crowd as best they could.

The official procession winding slowly through the principal streets was of course much longer in reaching the hotel, and when it finally arrived, the narrow corridors of the Bates House were jammed to a degree which made entrance almost impossible. After much effort Mr. Lincoln got to his room but was almost immediately called out to address the crowd from one of the balconies. During this and other preliminaries quite a little time slipped away when the President-elect suddenly remembered that little black carpetbag with its important contents. Robert was vehemently called for; but Robert's advance arrival had been discovered by "The Boys" who had hurried him off to see the city and his enthusiastic friends. He was finally discovered and brought in, and in answer to his father's more than pressing inquiries related that arriving in the confusion, unheralded, and having no room to go to, he knew of nothing better to do than to hand the carpetbag to the clerk of the hotel—after the usual manner of travelers.

"And what did the clerk do with it?" asked his father.

"Set it on the floor behind the counter," answered Robert complacently.

A look of stupefaction passed over the countenance of Mr. Lincoln, and visions of that Inaugural in all the next morning's newspapers floated through his imagination. Without a word he opened the door of his room, forced his way through the crowded corridor down to the office, where, with a single stride of his long legs, he swung himself across the clerk's counter, behind which a small mountain of carpetbags of all colors had accumulated. Then drawing a little key out of his pocket he began delving for the black ones, and opened one by one those that the key would unlock, to the great surprise and amusement of the clerk and bystanders, as their miscellaneous contents came to light. Fortune favored the President-elect, for after the first half dozen trials, he found his treasures. The somewhat stern admonition which Robert received, was compensated for by the fact that during the remainder of the trip he did not again have to carry that carpetbag, Mr. Lincoln carefully keeping it under his own hands and eyes.[47]

As Mr. Lincoln's journey progressed, his wisdom in making it one of public oration became apparent. The invitation of Legislatures had in every instance been tendered him by a non-partizan vote, and in all his public addresses he acknowledged and commended the fact, accepting the demonstrations of welcome as from the people to the Chief Magistrate and not to the man. Under the peculiar circumstances, however, the popular curiosity and feeling were as much concerning the man as the magistrate; for his whole bearing, manner, and utterance carried conviction to all beholders that the man was of them as well as for them. There is a power of fine discrimination in the eyes and ears of an intelligent American multitude that does not often fail to rightly interpret the personal relation of the official to the constituent. It is an art they have learned at their endless mass-meetings and conventions, if it is not the more subtle, psychological influence permeating human society, which exists though it may baffle all laws of proof and definition. If such a current of electrical communion from the people to Mr. Lincoln be denied or disproven, those who stood near him throughout this memorable journey can give earnest testimony to its presence from Mr. Lincoln to the people.

The first manifestation of it which his intimate friends experienced, was the trouble with committees. There was a committee of some sort at every station, at every stopping place, at every State line; while at every capital there were committees innumerable; from the Governor, from each branch of the Legislature, from bodies of Wide Awakes, from bodies of working men, from organizations of various sorts. They were all eager to see the President-elect, to shake his hand, to make speeches and ask him to reply, to invite him hither and thither; and all this in perfect sincerity, in genuine hospitality, in that irrepressible enthusiasm which only those anomalous and exciting times could generate.

His more intimate friends, in Mr. Lincoln's suite, were perhaps on their part over anxious for his personal comfort and safety, and were dismayed at the readiness with which, at the beginning, he placed himself under the leadership of such committees; for they quickly discovered that these committees were often composed of men utterly without that quick executive judgment which knew when to start and where and how to go. In the push and crush of these dense throngs of people, in this rushing of trains, clanging of bells, booming of guns, shouting and huzzas of individuals and crowds, it was difficult to instantly determine which call was the more important or more proper, and a false start might not only bring on an irretrievable waste of time and a derangement of official programmes and processions, but a false step even might bring danger to life or limb under wheels of locomotives or carriages. These committees generally seemed consumed by a demon of impatience. They would sometimes tumble pell-mell into a car and almost drag Mr. Lincoln out before the train had even stopped, and habitually, after stoppage, before the proper police or military guards could be stationed about a depot or stopping place to secure necessary space and order for a comfortable open path to the waiting carriages. For a time it seemed as though Mr. Lincoln could not resist the popular importunings. His sympathy with and for the people made him shrink, not as a matter of reasoning but apparently upon some constitutional impulse, from any objection to or protest against the over eagerness and over officiousness of these first greetings. It was not till after some days of experience and several incidents of discomfort that he conquered this impulse, but having mastered it he kept it for the remainder of the journey under perfect control, and would remain seated in his car until he received the notice agreed upon that preparations outside had been deliberately completed. But it was easy to note that this control of his kindly impulses caused him both effort and pain—that while his judgment made him resolutely refuse the popular call for his presence outside, his heart and feelings were with the enthusiastic and clamorous multitude.

The local committees everywhere, so far as Mr. Lincoln's time would permit, arranged evening receptions, generally at the hotel at which he was stopping, where the public at large, both ladies and gentlemen, might have the opportunity to pass by him and shake his hand. But these hand-shakings of two or three hours' duration added to the day's fatigue of travel and official ceremony, were found to be a serious tax upon his strength, and many of his friends urged him to stand where he might simply bow to the passers by and omit the handshaking. The experiment was tried two or three times but always with unsatisfactory results. To the curious individuals who were passing it seemed a performance and created an impression, ranging from the feeling on the one hand that they were assisting at an animal show, to that on the other, that they were engaged in a grotesque ceremony of mock adulation. To Mr. Lincoln it produced a consciousness not only of being on exhibition, but as if he were separated by an abyss from those with whom as fellow-citizens and constituents it was more than ever an imperative duty to be brought into closer relations and sympathy. Under such conditions the crowd could only pass by him, either with a meaningless smirk or an open-mouthed stare; no talk either of earnestness or pleasantry was possible. This was infinitely worse than the utmost fatigue, and Mr. Lincoln returned to the old custom where a cordial grasp of the hand and a fitting word formed an instantaneous circuit of personal communion. The custom is the practical symbol of American equality and brotherhood; if it is ever abandoned American society will have lost a quickening element of vitality.

His sympathy with the crowds of people who came to see him appeared in still another form. There were many way-stations where the train halted for a few moments, and at these points there was sure to be a considerable crowd, as indeed there also was at places where no stop was made. At all these temporary halts there would be lusty cheering and unceasing calls for Mr. Lincoln. It was of course impossible for him to make speeches everywhere, and yet no sooner would he make his appearance on the rear platform of the car than calls for a speech would come out of every throat. The people wanted not only to look upon their President-elect, but to hear his voice. If he had been of colder nature, he could of course have bowed and quickly retired into the car; but this it seemed impossible for him to do, at least to do with comfort to himself. There was a fascination upon him in these united appeals of an assemblage of American citizens, no matter of what State or what county and he could not easily wrench himself away from their eager faces and appealing voices without saying a few words. And to do this, there was the danger, on the one hand of merely repeating stale compliments, and on the other of uttering some opinion on public questions for which he was not yet ready. The expedient was therefore resorted to that he would remain inside until the conductor of the train should notify him that he was ready to start, so that when Mr. Lincoln stepped out of the door only time would be left to make two or three bows in different directions when the moving train would bear him away from his enthusiastic admirers while he was standing, hat in hand, upon the platform.

At Columbus, Ohio, Mr. Lincoln's friends had a chance to observe how necessary it was to look carefully to his personal surroundings at every moment. The magnificent State House in that city had recently been completed and the committee of arrangements had provided that after the morning ceremonies before the Legislature, an informal reception should take place in the afternoon, in the rotunda of the building or rather at the point of intersection where on the ground floor the two great public corridors cross each other. It was intended that there should be one entrance on one side, and the exit at the other side of the building, so that the people should pass through in a straight line. But an inadequate police force had been detailed to guard the entrance to the transverse corridor; these were soon forced open and a stream of humanity poured from the outside toward the center by the three large avenues, leaving only one for exit, and before anyone was well aware of the occurrence there was a concentric jam of the crowd toward the President-elect which threatened to crush him and those about him. Fortunately Colonel [*Ward Hill*] Lamon of his suite who was a man of extraordinary size and herculean strength, was able to place himself before him and by formidable exertion to hold back the advancing pressure until Mr.

Lincoln could be hurried to a more secure place behind the corner of a pilaster which projected a little more than the thickness of his person, and which thus formed a protecting barrier on two sides until the inflow at the entrance could be checked and regulated.

It was utterly impossible to make provisions against risks of this character, because no one could foresee the exact conditions under which they might occur. For instance the presidential train arrived in the depot at Pittsburg awhile after dark, and there were only a few gas jets here and there which served rather to intensify than to dispel the obscurity. The local committee had provided carriages, as usual, for the President and his party, but had somewhat complicated matters by stationing them, together with a small cavalry escort, entirely too near the tracks. When the train with its rush and noise, its steam whistle going, its bell ringing, moved into its place, the carriage and cavalry horses, many of them entirely unaccustomed to such a din, were seized with fright and a commotion among these animals took place which amounted to almost a stampede; and in the darkness and confusion the President-elect was compelled to find his carriage. His immediate friends clustered about him to render all possible assistance, under the gravest apprehension for his safety, themselves running much danger of personal injury from what at the moment was an absolutely uncontrolable mélé of moving wheels and hoofs, of noise and shouting, in a half light that confused correct judgment and baffled caution, permitting only the single vivid and realistic impression that chaos had come. It happened fortunately, that no accident occurred, but that result was certainly not due to favoring conditions of security.

The incidents of the arrival at Buffalo did not turn out quite so well. While Mr. Lincoln succeeded in reaching his carriage in safety, nearly everyone accompanying him underwent a terrible struggle with the crowd, and Major—afterward Major General—Hunter, of his suite, received an injury which compelled him to carry his arm in a sling for the remainder of the journey.[48] If the following description of occurrences at that place were written from memory simply, the writer might be suspected of drawing an extravagant picture. He therefore prefers to quote a report of the incidents printed two days afterwards in the Buffalo "Morning Express" of February 18, 1861:

Punctually at the appointed hour, 4:30 p.m., a salute from the cannon of Major Weidrich's Artillery Company, posted on Michigan Street, announced the approach of the train bearing the President-elect and his suite, and in a moment more it was within the depot. The wildest cheering greeted its arrival—cheering that began with the multitude away down the track of the railroad, gathering volume as it rolled up to the depot, and continued on through the mass extending far up the street, until it became a roar that was mightier and more majestic in sound than the boom of the cannon. Within the depot there was a fierce struggle among the crowd, striving to compress itself within view of the rear car of the train, which was understood to contain the President. By dint of great effort, "D" Company, which had been detached from the 74th Regiment to form an escort and guard for Mr. Lincoln, succeeded in opening a passage from the platform of the President's car to the main exit from the depot, and were ranged in line on each side of the same. A moment or two was consumed in making arrangements, when Mr. Lincoln appeared upon the platform of the car, accompanied by A. M. Clapp, Esq., Chairman of the Committee appointed to escort him from Cleveland to Buffalo. At the steps of the car Mr. Lincoln was met by Ex-President Fillmore, who, upon introduction, greeted him in a few words simply of congratulation upon the safety of his journey and the preservation of his health, in response to which Mr. Lincoln expressed his thanks. Attended there by Mr. Fillmore, Mr. Clapp, and Alderman Berrie, Mayor *pro tem*, the President proceeded to the carriage, through the line opened by the artillery.

The scene that took place upon the instant that Mr. Lincoln left the car, was one that we shall describe with regret and shame. The crowd, in its crazed eagerness to get nearer to the distinguished visitor—the man in whom circumstances have centered a deeper and more universal interest than ever was felt, perhaps, in any other living individual by the American people—became an ungoverned mob, making an irresistible rush towards him which swept the soldiers from their lines, and threw everything into the wildest confusion that we ever witnessed in our lives. We have seen masses of people in a great many exciting struggles; we have seen scrambles and commotions, and surging mobs of men, on a great many wild occasions, we have experienced the jam and pressure and sweeping, overwhelming force of agitated multitudes many a memorable time; but we never saw anything to compare with the fearful rush of this crowd after the President as he was leaving the depot. It was awful. Men were overcome with the pressure to the point of fainting. Some, whom we shall mention hereafter, were seriously injured. The soldiers, as we have said were overwhelmed in an instant, and their weapons came very near becoming deadly without intention. Several bayonets got lowered in the fierce struggle of the soldiery with the crowd, and were actually wedged into the living mass so firmly that they could not be extricated. In one instance, the point of a bayonet, sharp as a stiletto, pressed against the breast of a man, and there seemed for a moment no mode of saving him from being pierced by it. A dozen hands seized the bayonet and the musket to which it was attached, and it was only by a herculean effort that the deadly weapon was wrenched from its dangerous aim.

There were other instances of imminent peril from like causes which were scarcely less thrilling; and it is hardly to be comprehended how there was escape from more serious results than we have to report. Major Hunter, of the President's suite, received in some manner, from the tremendous pressure of the crowd, a sprain of the shoulder, so severe that it was at first thought to be a dislocation or a fracture. An old gentleman, named Bruce, from Lancaster, was so terribly jammed in the doorway, that he sank from the effects, and had to be conveyed into the Wadsworth House, where a medical attendant was summoned. We understand that several of his ribs were found to be displaced; but that the injury, though severe, is not dangerous. There were many in the crowd perfectly exhausted by the pressure and struggle, who escaped from it with a feeling of gratitude for the preservation of their lives.

The President, himself, we are happy to say, was saved from much pressure by a tremendous effort on the part of the military who succeeded in rallying around him, and was safely assisted to the carriage at the depot entrance. Members of his suite, and others accompanying him, were subject to much uncomfortable treatment.

It is a sincere pleasure to the writer to add that disorder of so serious a kind occurred on only three or four days out of the twelve occupied by the entire Presidential journey. At most of the places the preparations were reasonably satisfactory, and in a few of them as perfect, orderly, and quiet as is possible on occasions where the interest is so intense and where the crowds are so large. It is hard for anyone who has not had the chance of personal observation to realize the mingled excitement and apprehension, elation and fatigue which Mr. Lincoln and his suite underwent, almost without intermission for the period of nearly two weeks during this memorable trip from Springfield to Washington.

The departure from Buffalo on Monday at the early hour of five o'clock A.M. formed a vivid contrast to the turmoil and danger which had attended the arrival on Saturday. It was a grey, cold, dull winter morning, with snow on the ground, with silence, [   ] and spectral dawn outside, and gloom and ominous shadows dimly penetrated by a few feeble lamp-rays inside the depot, giving an air of unreality to the muffled or flitting forms, and the clanging and hissing sounds that came back in hollow echoes from walls and arches. But the train was soon in motion; and then the rapidly coming daylight, and the stations and villages that danced in quick succession past the car windows, by and by restored the usual routine; and the repeated scenes of the day are faithfully recorded in the newspaper report:

The vital history of that day's ride is to be written in three words: "Crowds, cannon and cheers." Such crowds—surging through long arches, cursing the military and blessing Old Abe; swinging hats, banners, handkerchiefs, and every possible variety of festival bunting; and standing with open mouths as the train, relentlessly punctual, moved away. The history of one is the history of all; depots in waves, as if the multitudinous sea had been let loose, and its billows transformed into patriots, clinging along roofs and balconies and pillars, fringing long embankments, swarming upon adjacent trains of motionless cars, shouting, bellowing, shrieking, howling; all were boisterous; all bubbling with patriotism. The enthusiasm for the President was spontaneous and universal; and when we reached Albany, everybody present congratulated himself that he had been a witness of one of the most memorable of triumphal processions which this or any other country has ever witnessed.[49]

Passing by the reception at Albany, which was a somewhat amplified repetition of those at Indianapolis and Columbus—speeches, and a dinner from the governor, speeches, and a dinner from the legislature—there is room only to mention that at the great city of New York which was reached on Tuesday afternoon the 19th, while the crowds were the largest encountered during the whole journey, the police arrangements were among the most perfect, and that neither accident nor inconvenience attended Mr. Lincoln's movement through the numerous "functions" which committees had prearranged. Broadway had been kept clear, so that the double line of carriages which made up the procession moved from the depot where the train arrived down the whole length of that magnificent street to the Astor House in perfect order and with plenty of room, giving to the people who crowded the side streets, doors, balconies, windows, and lined even the roofs of buildings with a continuous fringe of humanity, a clear view of the President-elect.

The speeches, the delegations, the hand-shakings, the serenades, need not be recounted; it will suffice to reprint the description of the visit of the President-elect to the Academy of Music while the first act of the Opera "The Masked Ball" was in progress:

At about a quarter past eight Mr. Lincoln, accompanied by Judge Davis of Illinois, and Alderman Cornell, entered, wholly unnoticed, the right hand proscenium box, on a line with the second tier.[50] Another party, including two ladies, took seats behind the distinguished visitor. The first act over, the audience, having discovered his arrival, applauded him loudly. Mr. Lincoln bowed his acknowledgment of this courtesy, and resumed his seat amid renewed enthusiasm. After the lapse of half a minute a second round of applause was elicited, accompanied by cheers and the waving of hats and handkerchiefs. The ladies evinced much curiosity and fluttered their fans and mouchoirs with patriotic fervor. Again Mr. Lincoln bowed and sat down. The efforts to obtain a speech failed, as was only proper it should, under the circumstances. The curtain now rose, and the entire company sang the "Star Spangled Banner", the audience rising en masse. Miss Phillips sang the solo stanzas correctly. At the end of the first stanza a magnificent American flag was suddenly dropped half way down to the floor from between the flies. The presidential party remained standing, as did the entire audience, until the good old tune was finished. The band played "Hail Columbia" as the curtain fell, after which the opera proceeded. The President and the gentlemen who attended him took their leave quietly at the close of the second act.

During the time thus far consumed by the presidential journey, another popular and political drama had been going on in the South. Rebellion had gradually culminated in the seven Cotton States, and a provisional Congress had met at Montgomery, Alabama. On the 8th of February, three days before Mr. Lincoln started from Springfield, that provisional Congress had adopted a provisional government of the "Confederate States"; and on the 18th, the day of Mr. Lincoln's arrival at Albany, Jefferson Davis had been inaugurated as the Confederate "President," with all the attendant popular display of a short railroad journey, demonstrations of welcome, speeches of prophetic greatness of the independent South, and holiday jubilation at Montgomery. Enthusiasm was abundant and earnest; but in the essential elements of territory, population, cities, wealth, agricultural resources, mechanical power, passed in review, and represented and tendered by loyal acclamation, the insurrectionary manifestations were to the magnificent sweep of Mr. Lincoln's triumphal procession from the great West to the great East but as the ripples on a mill-pond to the groundswell of the sea.

In the light of after occurrences we can now see that the President-elect correctly divined and interpreted the events of each day both at the South and at the North, during his memorable journey. After leaving New York, while his replies to addresses were in the same general spirit and language, one or two phrases which seemed prompted by momentary impulse rather than studied premeditation gave evidence of a feeling of graver responsibility and more determined resolution than had hitherto colored his words. His little speech at Trenton to the Assembly of New Jersey contained a sentence showing that he did not disguise to himself the significance of the proceedings and incidents at Montgomery. "The man does not live," he said, "who is more devoted to peace than I am—none who would do more to preserve it—but it may be necessary to put the foot down firmly," and the loud and continued cheering which greeted the intimation must have convinced him that he had struck the keynote of the popular will of the North.

So, again, in the remarks made by him in Independence Hall in Philadelphia, and before the Pennsylvania Legislature in Harrisburg while earnestly deprecating war and bloodshed, there was an undertone of promise that the government and institutions of the country should be maintained, the flag of the Union be kept "flaunting gloriously," and the sentiment of the Declaration of Independence be perpetuated. How faithfully he kept that promise need not be recounted here.

NOTES
INDEX

NOTES

EDITOR'S INTRODUCTION

1. Undated article by Jess M. Thompson, "Nicolay Was German Citizen," clipping from an unidentified Pittsfield newspaper in the Carl Sandburg Collection, Illinois Historical Survey, University of Illinois Library; Thomas Hall Shastid, *My Second Life: An Autobiography* (Ann Arbor, Mich.: George Wahr, 1944), 63. Shastid heard this story from Mrs. Garbutt on many occasions.

2. Sent by Nicolay on 17 November 1887 to the editors of the *Dizionario Bigraphico degli Scrittori Contemporanei*. Copy, Nicolay Papers, Library of Congress.

3. Thompson, "Nicolay Was German Citizen," Carl Sandburg Collection, Illinois Historical Survey, University of Illinois Library.

4. Shastid, *My Second Life*, 72n.

5. Shastid, *My Second Life*, 71.

6. "Lincoln in Early Life, Colonel Nicolay's Reminiscences," Washington correspondence by C., 2 December 1887, *Chicago Herald*, 4 December 1887.

7. Undated memorandum by Nicolay, "dictated to Helen M. Hough," Nicolay Papers, Library of Congress.

8. Robert Todd Lincoln to Isaac Markens, Manchester, Vt., 4 November 1917, Robert Todd Lincoln Papers, Chicago Historical Society.

9. Statement by Messrs. McKee and Fishback, proprietors of the *Missouri Democrat*, 3 September 1857, Nicolay Papers, Library of Congress.

10. Lincoln to Greeley, Springfield, 8 November 1858, in Roy P. Basler et al., eds., *The Collected Works of Abraham Lincoln*, 9 vols. (New Brunswick: Rutgers University Press, 1953–55), 3:336.

11. Nicolay to Hatch, 21 December 1859, and George M. Parsons to Lincoln, 17 January 1860, in David C. Mearns, ed., *The Illinois Political Campaign of 1858: A Facsimile of the Printer's Copy of his Debates with Senator Stephen Arnold Douglas as Edited and Prepared for Press by Abraham Lincoln* (Washington: Library of Congress, n. d.), 9–10.

12. Undated memorandum by Nicolay, "dictated to Helen M. Hough," Nicolay Papers, Library of Congress. In 1887 Nicolay told a journalist how he had been disappointed about not getting the commission to write a campaign biography of Lincoln: "I was regretting my bad luck a day or two later to Mr. [*William*] Butler, a close friend of Lincoln's, when he interrupted me with, 'Hush, that's of no consequence. You are to be private secretary.' " "Lincoln in Early Life, Colonel Nicolay's Reminiscences," Washington correspondence by C., *Chicago Herald*, 4 December 1887.

13. A. S. Chapman, "The Boyhood of John Hay," *Century Magazine*, n.s., 46 (July 1909), 452.

14. Among those receiving copies were D. W. Bartlett, William Dean Howells, and Scripps. Nicolay to Jesse W. Weik, Washington, 13 February 1895, copy, Nicolay Papers, Library of Congress.

15. Kreismann to Charles H. Ray, Washington, 16 December 1860, Ray Papers, Huntington Library, San Marino, Calif.

16. William O. Stoddard, "White House Sketches," No. II, *New York Citizen*, 25 August 1866, and *Inside the White House in War Times* (New York: Charles L. Webster, 1890), 104. In the latter work, Stoddard says: "people who do not like him [*Nicolay*]—because they cannot use him, perhaps—say he is sour and crusty, and it is a grand good thing, then, that he is. If you will sit in that chair a month or so, you will see what has become of any easy good-nature you sat down with. . . . The President showed his good judgment of men when he put Mr. Nicolay just where he is, with a kind and amount of authority which it is not easy to describe."

17. Robert Colby to Lincoln, New York, 18 May 1861, Lincoln Papers, Library of Congress.

18. "The Defeat of Hamlin," *Washington Post*, 9 July 1891.

19. Young, "Lincoln as He Was," *Pittsburgh Dispatch*, 23 August 1891.

20. John G. Nicolay and John Hay, *Abraham Lincoln: A History*, 10 vols. (New York: Century, 1890). The biography has not worn well. Allan Nevins dismissed it as "an appalling mixture of history and biography, the history now being completely outdated, and the biography so fulsome in its flattery, so blind to all Lincoln's shortcomings and defects as he grew up into greatness, that it is now almost worthless. . . . " Nevins to Ida M. Tarbell, New York, 30 May 1939, Tarbell Papers, Allegheny College. See also Benjamin P. Thomas, *Portrait for Posterity: Lincoln and His Biographers* (New Brunswick, N.J.: Rutgers University Press, 1947), 128–29.

21. Hay to Nicolay, 22 November 1872, in Tyler Dennett, *John Hay: From Poetry to Politics* (New York: Dodd, Meade, 1934), 134.

22. "In the afternoon John G. Nicolay, formerly Mr. Lincoln's private Secretary, called at my room and had about two hours conversation with me in regard to Mr Lincoln, making memorandums as we talked." Browning's diary entry, 17 June 1875, in Theodore Calvin Pease and James G. Randall, eds., *The Diary of Orville Hickman Browning* (2 vols.; Collections of the Illinois State Historical Library, Vols. 20 and 22; Springfield: Illinois State Historical Library, 1925, 1933), 2:415.

23. "I send you today . . . a lot of manuscript notes of my Springfield interviews. . . . I found upon examining my notes that I would do better to write them out myself—that to use a phonographer I would waste about as much time in directing him how to paragraph and punctuate as I would be likely to gain." Nicolay to Hay, Washington, 16 November 1875, Hay Papers, Brown University.

24. Lincoln wrote to Justice David Davis of the Supreme Court: "I wished particularly to say a word for our good friend Mr. Nicolay. I sincerely trust you can find it possible to aid him. You as well as nearly all the Justices knew him when he was here with my father, & I think no one could question his great personal fitness for the place. In so far as my poor word could assist him, I give it with the earnest hope

he may succeed." Robert Todd Lincoln to David Davis, Washington, 28 November 1872, David Davis Papers, Illinois State Historical Library, Springfield.

25. Helen Nicolay, *Personal Traits of Abraham Lincoln* (New York: Century, 1912). A handful of Nicolay's interviews are located in the Illinois State Historical Library in Springfield.

26. Nicolay to Robert Todd Lincoln, Washington, 3 March 1874, copy, Nicolay Papers, Library of Congress.

27. Ida M. Tarbell, *All in the Day's Work: An Autobiography* (New York: Macmillan, 1939), 161–63.

28. In 1885 Stoddard sent John Hay a copy of the second edition of his Lincoln biography and asked for comments and criticisms. "Nicolay has not left me at liberty to write to him or to send him a copy &c," he added. A month later Stoddard told Hay,

> I did not suppose I was crossing your track or "taking away your market," and so said in my preface. I have left that unchanged in the edition now going out. Long ago I wrote you and Nicolay that I had a book in my mind and it was my idea, year after year, that yours would come out first. Is it too much to say that that idea died of old age? I hope you will make as full and valuable a work as I have thought of your making and that it will succeed *enormously*. Mine seems to find its place. So will yours. I have certainly done something in the way of advertising you. Never mind if your note nettled me a little but I certainly have not intentionally stolen a march on anybody. (Stoddard to Hay, New York, 12 February and 25 March 1885, Hay Papers, Brown University)

29. Hay to Charles Francis Adams, Washington, 19 December 1903, Hay Papers, Brown University. Major Thomas T. Eckert, chief of the War Department telegraph staff, and Assistant Secretary of War Charles A. Dana, who were both with Lincoln on election night in November 1864, denied that Hay had been present. *New York Sun*, n.d., copied in an unidentified clipping, "A Curious Story of Lincoln," John Hay scrapbook, vol. 62, Hay Papers, Library of Congress. Hay replied to Dana, quoting from his diary that showed that he was, in fact, present. Dana in the *New York Sun*, 1 January 1890. In 1891 Hay complained to Nicolay: "Every old dead-beat politician in the country is coming forward to protest that he was the depository of Lincoln's inmost secrets and the engineer of his campaign. And every one of them, whom we have not mentioned, is thirsting for our gore." Hay to Nicolay, Cleveland, 25 July 1891, copy, Nicolay Papers, Library of Congress.

30. Nicolay and Hay, *Lincoln*, 1:xiii; Nicolay to Roswell Smith, Washington, 22 January 1889, copy, Nicolay Papers, Library of Congress; Hay to Buel, Newbury, N. H., 14 September 1895, Hay Papers, Brown University; Hay to Richard Watson Gilder, Cleveland, 13 August 1885, Lincoln File, Huntington Library, San Marino, Calif.

31. R. T. Lincoln did censor Nicolay and Hay's work. See the manuscript of the

opening chapters of volume 1, Nicolay-Hay Papers, Illinois State Historical Library, Springfield.

32. An exception is the Stephen T. Logan interview, most of which was published in the *Abraham Lincoln Centennial Association Bulletin,* no. 12 (1 September 1928), 1–3, 5.

33. Nicolay and Hay, *Lincoln,* 1:201.

34. Milton Hay to John Hay, Springfield, 8 February 1887, Hay Papers, Brown University.

35. Douglas L. Wilson, "Abraham Lincoln and 'That Fatal First of January,' " *Civil War History* 38, no. 2 (June 1992), 101–30; Michael Burlingame, *The Inner World of Abraham Lincoln* (Urbana: University of Illinois Press, 1994), 99–102, 315.

36. Nicolay to Richard Watson Gilder, Washington, 17 February 1894, Small Manuscripts Collection, no. 1107, Illinois State Historical Library, Springfield. In addition to the two essays reproduced in this volume, Nicolay submitted one entitled "Lincoln in Politics," which was published by the McClure's syndicate on 10 February 1895. Gilder rejected the latter and asked Nicolay to condense the other two essays for possible publication. Gilder to Nicolay, 2 March 1894, Nicolay Papers, Library of Congress. Gilder did publish the following essays by Nicolay in *The Century:* "Lincoln's Personal Appearance" (October 1891), "Lincoln's Gettysburg Address" (February 1894), and "Lincoln's Literary Experiments" (April 1894).

37. William Allen White, *A Puritan in Babylon: The Story of Calvin Coolidge* (New York: Macmillan, 1938), vii, quoted in Donald Ritchie, *Doing Oral History* (New York: Twayne, 1995), 14.

38. James G. Randall, *Lincoln the President: Springfield to Gettysburg,* 2 vols. (New York: Dodd, Mead, 1945), 2:324–25.

39. Douglas L. Wilson, "Abraham Lincoln, Ann Rutledge, and the Evidence of Herndon's Informants," *Civil War History* 36 (December 1990), 321. See also Wilson, "William H. Herndon and His Lincoln Informants," *Journal of the Abraham Lincoln Association* 14 (winter 1993), 15–34, and "William H. Herndon and the "Necessary Truth," in George L. Painter, ed., *Abraham Lincoln in the American Mind* (Springfield: Lincoln Home National Historical Site, 1994), 31–41.

40. Ritchie, *Doing Oral History,* 92.

41. Joseph Bucklin Bishop, *Notes and Anecdotes of Many Years* (New York: Scribner's, 1925), 5.

1. THE SPRINGFIELD INTERVIEWS

1. Hay Papers, Brown University. Orville H. Browning (1806–81) first met Lincoln in the mid-1830s, and from that time till 1865, Browning said, "our relations were very intimate: I think more so than is usual. Our friendship was close, warm, and, I believe, sincere. I know mine for him was, and I never had reason to distrust his for me. Our relations, to my knowledge, were never interrupted for a moment."

Browning to Isaac N. Arnold, Quincy, Ill., 25 November 1872, Arnold Papers, Chicago Historical Society.

One historian maintained that Browning "was Lincoln's life-long associate in law and politics, his cherished adviser and his intimate friend—hardly anyone [was] closer to him. . . . " Harlan Hoyt Horner, "Lincoln Rebukes a Senator," *Journal of the Illinois State Historical Society* 44 (1951), 116. Browning served in the Illinois Senate for four years (1836–40), while Lincoln sat in the state house of representatives. They lodged at the same house and spent much time together. From July 1861 to January 1863, Browning was a U.S. senator and visited the White House almost daily while Congress was in session. Maurice Baxter, *Orville Hickman Browning: Lincoln's Friend and Critic* (Bloomington: Indiana University Press, 1957); Theodore Calvin Pease, introduction to Pease and Randall, *Diary of Browning*, 1:xi–xxxii.

Browning was critical of Lincoln in 1864, when he told a friend: "I am personally attached to the President, and have faithfully tried to uphold him, and make him respectable, tho' I never have been able to persuade myself that he was big enough for his position. Still, I thought he might get through, as many a boy has got through College, without disgrace, and without knowledge, but I fear he is a failure." Browning to (Edgar) Cowan, Quincy, Ill., 6 September 1864, photostatic copy, James G. Randall Papers, Library of Congress.

2. In January 1841, just after he had broken his engagement to Mary Todd, Lincoln was deeply depressed. On the subject of Lincoln's depressions, see Burlingame, *Inner World of Lincoln*, 92–122.

3. William Butler (1797–1876), clerk of the Sangamon County Circuit Court (1836–41), befriended Lincoln when he served in the state legislature. See the interviews with Butler elsewhere in this volume. He became Illinois state treasurer in 1859. Herndon maintained that Lincoln boarded for free with Butler from 1837 to 1842. Herndon to Weik, 16 January 1886, Herndon-Weik Papers, Library of Congress. Cf. William J. Butler (grandson of William Butler), "Butler Helped Mold Lincoln's Life," *Illinois State Journal* (Springfield), 28 February 1937, part 4, 11; John G. Nicolay, "Lincoln's Personal Appearance," *The Century Magazine* 42, no. 6 (October 1891), 936.

4. Ninian W. Edwards (1809–89), son of the governor of Illinois, married Elizabeth Todd, Mary Todd's eldest sister. In the autumn of 1839, Mary Todd left her home in Kentucky to live with her sister and brother-in-law. Edwards, according to an Illinois Democrat, "had inherited from his father so much vanity and egotism that it made him offensive to most of his acquaintances. . . . Naturally and constitutionally an aristocrat . . . he hated democracy as the devil is said to hate holy water." Usher F. Linder, quoted in Paul Simon, *Lincoln's Preparation for Greatness: The Illinois Legislative Years* (Norman: University of Oklahoma Press, 1965), 47.

5. Robert Smith Todd was Mary's father. Mary, apparently, did not get along with her stepmother. Burlingame, *Inner World of Lincoln*, 270, 293–94.

6. Her friend Margaret Stuart said that as a youngster, Mary Todd was "very

highly strung, nervous, impulsive, excitable, having an emotional temperament much like an April day, sunning all over with laughter one moment, the next crying as though her heart would break." Katherine Helm, *The True Story of Mary, Wife of Lincoln* (New York: Harper, 1928), 32.

7. Matilda Rachel Edwards (1824–51) married Newton D. Strong in 1846. They had no children.

8. See Wilson, "Fatal First of January," 101–30; William H. Herndon to Ward Hill Lamon, Springfield, 25 February 1870, Lamon Papers, Huntington Library, San Marino, Calif.; two essays by H. O. Knerr, both entitled "Abraham Lincoln and Matilda Edwards," Ida M. Tarbell Papers, Allegheny College; Knerr in the *Allentown (Penn.) Morning Call*, 9 February 1936. A niece of one of Mary Todd Lincoln's sisters said, "It was always known in our family . . . that Mr. Lincoln courted Matilda Edwards, a fact which for many reasons she divulged only to her nearest and dearest." Horace Green, "Mother's Appeal Granted," unidentified clipping, Lincoln Museum, Fort Wayne, Ind. According to a young woman in Springfield at the time, Lincoln

had addressed Mary Todd and she accepted him and they had been engaged some time when a Miss Edwards of Alton came here, and he fell desperately in love with her and found he was not so much attached to Mary as he thought. He says if he had it in his power he would not have one feature of her face altered, he thinks she is so perfect (that is, Miss E.) He and Mr. Speed have spent the most of their time at [*the home of Ninian and Elizabeth*] Edwards this winter and Lincoln could never bear to leave Miss Edward's side in company. Some of his friends thought he was acting very wrong and very imprudently and told him so. . . . (Jane D. Bell to Anne Bell, Springfield, 27 January 1841, copy, James G. Randall Papers, Library of Congress)

9. Mary Todd's sister, Elizabeth Edwards, told Herndon that Lincoln, at the time he broke the engagement, "declared he hated Mary and loved Miss [*Matilda*] Edwards." It is not clear from Mrs. Edwards's account if Lincoln made this statement to Mary Todd. Mrs. Edwards's undated statement to Herndon, Herndon-Weik Papers, Library of Congress.

10. Lincoln told John J. Hardin "that he thought he did not love her [*Mary Todd*] as he should and that he would do her a great wrong if he married her." Interview with Mrs. Alexander R. McKee (née Martinette Hardin), "A Romance of Lincoln," by Marietta Holdstock Brown, clipping identified as "Indianapolis, 1896," Lincoln Museum, Fort Wayne, Ind. In early 1841, Lincoln said to Mrs. William Butler, "it would just kill me to marry Mary Todd." Sarah Rickard, sister of Mrs. Butler, interviewed by Nellie Crandall Sanford, *Kansas City Star*, 10 February 1907.

11. Newton Deming Strong (1809–66), a lawyer in Alton, was originally from Connecticut. He graduated from Yale in 1831, taught briefly at his alma mater (1834–

35), then moved to Alton. There he practiced law with Lewis Baldwin Parsons and was elected to the Illinois House of Representatives in 1844. In 1846 he married Matilda Edwards and moved to Reading, Pennsylvania, where he practiced law with his brother, William Strong (1808–95), who became an associate justice of the U.S. Supreme Court. Newton Strong spent his final years in St. Louis.

12. In fact, Lincoln suffered a debilitating attack of melancholy in 1835, when Ann Rutledge died. John Y. Simon, "Abraham Lincoln and Ann Rutledge," *Journal of the Abraham Lincoln Association* 11 (1990), 13–33.

13. Lincoln had good reason for such fears. See Michael Burlingame, *Honest Abe, Dishonest Mary* (Racine: Lincoln Fellowship of Wisconsin, 1994).

14. Thomas Hood (1799–1845), author of *The Haunted House*, among other works.

15. On April 25, 1862, Browning wrote in his diary:

At night I went to the Presidents. He was alone and complaining of head ache. Our conversation turned upon poetry, and each of us quoted a few lines from Hood. He asked me if I remembered the Haunted House. I replied that I had never read it. He rang his bell—sent for Hood's poems and read the whole of it to me, pausing occasionally to comment on passages which struck him as particularly felicitous. His reading was admirable and his criticisms evinced a high and just appreciation of the true spirit of poetry. He then sent for another volume of the same work, and read me that "lost heir," and then the "Spoilt Child" the humour of both of which he greatly enjoyed. I remained with [*him*] about an hour & a half, and left in high spirits, and a very genial mood; but as he said a crowd was buzzing about the door like bees, ready to pounce upon him as soon as I should take my departure, and bring him back to a realization of the annoyances and harrassments of his position. (Pease and Randall, *Diary of Browning*, 1:542–43)

16. The month before this interview took place, a jury adjudged Mary Todd Lincoln insane and she was committed to an asylum. She was declared sane in June 1876.

17. Ward Hill Lamon, *The Life of Abraham Lincoln: From His Birth to His Inauguration as President* (Boston: Osgood & Co., 1872).

18. Sally Logan, daughter of Stephen T. Logan (Lincoln's second law partner), married Lamon in 1861.

19. John J. Hardin (1810–47), a political ally and rival of Lincoln's; Stephen A. Douglas (1813–61); Edward D. Baker (1811–61), Lincoln's close friend, colleague at the bar, and political ally and rival.

20. Browning here conflates the legislative sessions of 1836–37 and 1837–38. He told Isaac N. Arnold,

In the winter of 1836-7 we were all at Vandalia, then the seat of government of this State. I was a member of the Senate, and Mr Lincoln of the House of Representatives. He and I had been previously acquainted, but he then first made the acquaintance of Mrs Browning. We all boarded at the same house. He was very fond of Mrs Browning's society, and spent many of his evenings, and much of his leisure time, at our rooms. We were all there together, again, in the winter of 1837-8, the same relations subsisting between us as during the preceding winter. After our return home, in the Spring of 1838, the letter in question was received. (Browning to Arnold, Quincy, Ill., 25 November 1872, Arnold Papers, Chicago Historical Society)

21. The young lady was Mary Owens (1808-77).

22. Lincoln to Mrs. Browning (née Elizabeth Caldwell), Springfield, 1 April 1838, in Basler et al., *Collected Works of Lincoln*, 1:117-19.

23. William Makepeace Thayer (1820-98), author of many books, including *The Bobbin Boy, or, How Nat Got His Learning, an Example for Youth* (1860). His book on Lincoln is *The Pioneer Boy, and How He Became President* (Boston: Walker, Wise, 1863).

24. In 1872 Isaac N. Arnold asked Browning about Lincoln's religious views. Browning replied: "Of his religious opinions I am not able to speak. It is more than probable we have conversed upon religious subjects; but, if we did, I am not able to call back to my recollection anything which was said in such conversations, with such distinctness as to warrant me repeating it. He held a pew in the [New York Avenue] Presbyterian Church, of which Rev Dr Gurley was pastor, and often attended service there." (Phineas D. Gurley [1816-68] was also chaplain of the U.S. Senate; he was at Lincoln's bedside when the president died and delivered the eulogy at his funeral.) Browning continued:

[*Lincoln*] not infrequently sent his carriage, of Sunday mornings, with a request that I would accompany him and Mrs Lincoln to church. Sometimes, after services were over, I would return with them to the White House to dinner, and spend the afternoon with him in the Library. On such occasions I have seen him reading the Bible, but never knew of his engaging in any other act of devotion. He did not invoke a blessing at table, nor did he have family prayers. What private religious devotions may have been customary with him I do not know. I have no knowledge of any.

At the time of his little son Willie's death [*20 February 1862*], Mrs Browning and I were out of the city, but returned to Washington on the evening of the same day of his death. The President and Mrs Lincoln sent their carriage for us immediately upon learning that we were in the city, and we went to the White House, and remained with them about a week. His son Tad was also very ill at the time, and I watched with him several consecutive nights. The President was in the room with me a portion of each night. He was in very deep distress at the loss of Willie, and agitated with apprehensions of a fatal termination of Tad's illness; but what "his religious views and feelings were" I do not know. I heard no expression of them. My impression is that, during the time I remained at the White House, on this occasion, he had several interviews with Rev Dr Gurley, but what occurred between them never came to my knowledge. Dr Gurley is now dead, and I am unable to say whether he left any record of his conferences with the President.

I know that Mr Lincoln was a firm believer in a superintending and overruling Providence, and in super-natural agencies and events. I know that he believed the destinies of men were, or, at least, that his own destiny was, shaped, and controlled, by an intelligence and power higher and greater than his own, and which he could neither control nor thwart. To what extent he believed in the revelations and miracles of the Bible and Testament, or whether he believed in them at all, I am not prepared to say; but I do know that he was not a scoffer at religion. During our long and intimate acquaintance and intercourse, I have no recollection of ever having heard an irreverent word fall from his lips. (Browning to Isaac N. Arnold, Quincy, Ill., 25 November 1872, Arnold Papers, Chicago Historical Society)

25. Lincoln was the guest of Indiana Governor Oliver P. Morton (1823–77) for breakfast on 12 February, the second day of his trip to Washington in 1861.

26. Browning to Lincoln, Quincy, Ill., 17 February 1861, Lincoln Papers, Library of Congress.

27. See Pease and Randall, *Diary of Browning.*

28. Hay Papers, Brown University. Attorney John Todd Stuart (1807–85), Lincoln's first law partner, was a mentor to Lincoln in both politics and law. Cf. Stuart's interview with James Quay Howard, ca. May 1860, Lincoln Papers, Library of Congress. A small portion of that interview appears in Roy P. Basler, ed., "James Quay Howard's Notes on Lincoln," *Abraham Lincoln Quarterly* 4, no. 8 (December 1947), 386–400. The handwritten version of that interview at the Library of Congress is virtually illegible; a clean copy in Nicolay's hand can be found in the Hay Papers, Brown University. See also Stuart's interviews in the Herndon-Weik Papers, Library of Congress.

29. In their account of the Black Hawk war, Nicolay and Hay relied heavily on the reminiscences of George Harrison and little on what Stuart says here. See *Lincoln,* 1:87–100. Attorney Thomas Moffett, a justice of the peace in Sangamon County, served in the 4th Regiment of J. D. Henry's 3rd Illinois Brigade.

30. Lincoln had been mustered in at New Salem on 21 April 1832 with a unit that contained many of his friends. On 22 April they arrived in Beardstown and on 30 April the militia set up a camp about four miles from Rushville. Lincoln was cho-

sen captain at Dallas Scott's farm on Richland Creek, approximately nine miles from New Salem.

31. The election took place on 6 August; Lincoln returned around 19 July.

32. George Forquer (1794–1837), half brother to Governor Thomas Ford, was a surveyor, speculator, and merchant who, after failing in business, became a lawyer and politician. He first won election to the Illinois House of Representatives from Monroe County in 1824 and then to the Illinois Senate from Sangamon County in 1832. Governor Edward Coles appointed him secretary of state. See Milo Milton Quaife, ed., *Ford's History of Illinois from 1818 to 1847*, 2 vols. (Chicago: Lakeside Press, 1946), 1:xviii–xix.

After Forquer had abandoned the Whigs for the Democrats, he became Register of the Land Office. During the political campaign of 1836, Lincoln ridiculed him. When Forquer delivered a "slasher-gaff" speech, full of sarcasm, Lincoln replied in kind. Noting that Forquer owned a house in Springfield with a lightning rod, Lincoln said mockingly: "I would rather die now, than, like the gentleman, change my politics, and simultaneous with the change receive an office worth $3,000 per year, and then have to erect a lightning-rod over my house to protect a guilty conscience from an offended God." Joshua F. Speed, *Reminiscences of Abraham Lincoln and Notes of a Visit to California: Two Lectures* (Louisville, Ky.: John P. Morton, 1884), 17–18.

33. The first issue of the *Sangamo Journal* appeared on 10 November 1831, edited by Simeon Francis (1796–1872) and his brother. The office was a brick structure at the intersection of Washington and Fifth streets in Springfield.

34. In fact, Lincoln did not serve in the 1831 Black Hawk campaign.

35. The militia was in Rock Island 7–10 May and reached Dixon's Ferry on 12 May. Word that Major Isiah Stillman's unit had been slaughtered reached them at Dixon's Ferry on 15 May. The brigade arrived at the battleground later the same day and left the following day after burying the dead. On 27 May they disbanded at Fort Johnson in Ottawa.

36. Iles (1796–1883), one of the original settlers of Springfield, was a prominent merchant and landowner in the town he helped found. Lincoln and seventy-one other militia joined the new unit.

37. Virginia-born John Dawson (ca. 1791–?) of Sangamon County, a veteran of the War of 1812, served in the legislature with Lincoln. A "spy battalion" was a unit of reconnaissance scouts. Stuart's chronology, however, is confused. In the margin, Nicolay wrote: "Maj. S. does not seem to be at all reliable about his dates."

38. The actual date was 1832.

39. Major John Dement (1804–83) of Vandalia had been defeated by Black Hawk on 25 June at Kellogg's Grove. He served as state treasurer (1831–36) and was a Democratic member of the Illinois House of Representatives (1828–31, 1836–37). Stuart's regiment reached Galena on 19 June.

40. Iles's company was mustered out on 16 June; Lincoln and some others then

joined a company of scouts commanded by Captain Jacob M. Early (1806–38). The period of enlistment was actually thirty days.

41. Early's company crossed into Wisconsin (then part of the Michigan Territory) on 1 July and was mustered out on 10 July.

42. William Miller, who served in the Black Hawk War, thought Lincoln's command "was the hardest set of men he ever saw." B. F. Irwin to William H. Herndon, 22 September 1866, in Albert J. Beveridge, *Abraham Lincoln: 1809–1858*, 2 vols. (Boston: Houghton Mifflin, 1928), 1:121. The Clary's Grove boys were a hell-raising, rough-and-tumble set of young men who occupied a site southwest of New Salem that had first been settled by John Clary in 1819.

43. James D. Henry (ca. 1794–1834), a Springfield storekeeper and the sheriff of Sangamon County, became a hero in the war. According to Paul M. Angle, Henry "exhibited real military capacity where the other commanders, of the regulars as well as the militia, exhibited a lamentable lack of it. Almost overnight he became a hero. A local poet celebrated his exploits in verse,

Brave Henry, foremost in the fight,
To him we owe the meed of might.
The Bard his deeds should tell,
And proud our Sangamo should be
That boasts a warrior such as he!

while upon his return to Springfield the citizens honored him and the officers under his command with a public ball at Miller's Hotel." *"Here I Have Lived": A History of Lincoln's Springfield* (Chicago: Abraham Lincoln Bookshop, 1971), 39.

44. Dr. George M. Harrison (1813–73), a messmate of Lincoln's in Jabob Early's company, described his experiences with Lincoln in an undated letter to William Herndon, Herndon-Weik Papers, Library of Congress. Harrison, like Lincoln, had his horse stolen the night before they were to leave for home.

45. A long-time friend and patron of Stephen A. Douglas, Murray McConnel (1798–1869) of Jacksonville was a wealthy landowner. He won election to the Illinois House of Representatives in 1832 and to the state senate in 1846. He became the fifth auditor of the U.S. Treasury in 1855. Attorney Alfred W. Cavarly (1793–1876), a Democrat from Carrollton, won election to the Illinois House of Representatives in 1826 and 1840 and to the state senate in 1842, 1844, and 1846. Lincoln debated him in March 1844 at Springfield. He took Edward D. Baker as his law partner. Peter Green of Clay County won election to the Illinois House of Representatives in 1836, 1838, 1840, and 1842.

Attorney William L. May (ca. 1793–1849) served in the Illinois House of Representatives in the late 1820s and later in the U.S. House of Representatives (1834–39). President Jackson appointed him receiver of public moneys for the United States Land Office in Springfield; in 1841 he became mayor of that city. "A greater compound of meanness and stupidity was never mingled," said one critic in 1834. "May was accused of having been guilty of a burglary a few years since. This charge was published in a newspaper. He immediately wrote to some of his friends who were acquainted with the transaction, and published a reply from one of them, which stated that at the time of the trial, it was the general impression that he (May) did not enter the House in the night time with a design to commit murder, but for the sake of an illicit intercourse with some female there. This, Mr. May published as his defense, and called upon the people to overlook the follies of his youth!" B. Willis to Artemas Hale, December 26, 1834, Illinois State Historical Library, Springfield, quoted in Simon, *Lincoln's Preparation for Greatness*, 19. In 1844 Lincoln humiliated May in a political debate at Peoria. Burlingame, *Inner World of Lincoln*, 153.

Thomas Ford (1800–1850) was elected governor of Illinois in 1842. He later wrote *The History of Illinois, From Its Commencement as a State in 1818 to 1847*. Peter Cartwright (1785–1872), a prominent Methodist clergyman, won election to the state legislature in 1828 and 1832. Lincoln defeated him for Congress in 1846.

46. A strong supporter of Stephen A. Douglas, Edmund Dick Taylor (1802–91) was a Springfield merchant from Virginia. He served in the Illinois legislature (1830–35) and became receiver of public moneys in Chicago in 1835. He eventually broke with the Douglas over the 1854 Kansas-Nebraska bill. Virginia-born Achilles Morris (d. 1847) of Sangamon County was elected to the Illinois House of Representatives in 1832. He was killed in the Mexican War.

47. Lincoln received 277 out of 300 votes.

48. Lincoln was clerking in Denton Offutt's store.

49. The home of Samuel Danley (born ca. 1780 in Pennsylvania) was the site of the Fancy Creek election in 1827. (I am grateful to Dr. Wayne C. Temple for tracking down the identity of Danley in the Illinois State Archives.) Clear Lake was a pond, fed by springs, almost one mile long and approximately three-quarters of a mile wide, about six miles east of Springfield. During the Civil War the site became Camp Butler, where many recruits were trained.

50. Stuart told James Quay Howard in 1860: "In 1834 he [*Lincoln*] was a candidate of the whigs for state legislature and was elected. During this canvass Lincoln and I met at what was called in those times a 'Beef-shooting.' There being several candidates for legislature, and my own election being conceded, some disaffected ones of my own party took L to the one side and told him they would transfer votes enough from me to him to elect him, if he would agree to it. Lincoln immediately took me behind a bush and told me of the dishonest proposition, and declared he would not consent to it for any office." Copy of Howard's notes of an interview with Stuart, ca. May 1860 Hay Papers, Brown University.

51. In 1834 Richard Quinton received 1,038 votes and finished fifth, and thus failed to win a seat; Stuart won 1,164 votes and finished fourth, thus securing a seat. Lincoln came in second with 1,376 votes. Cf. Nicolay and Hay, *Lincoln*, 1:121–22.

52. Hay Papers, Brown University.

53. Vermont-born Gurdon Saltonstall Hubbard (1802–86) was elected a representative from Danville in Vermilion County in 1832; the following year he moved

to Chicago, where he became a prominent Republican and businessman. He urged the legislature to forget about the proposed Illinois and Michigan Canal and instead build a railroad. See Hubbard's reminiscences of Lincoln in the legislature in Francis Fisher Browne, *The Every-Day Life of Abraham Lincoln* (Minneapolis: Northwestern Publishing, 1887), 126–27.

54. Sidney Breese (1800–1878), a prominent Democrat who represented Illinois in the U.S. Senate (1843–49), was regarded as the originator of the Illinois Central Railroad.

55. The canal bill passed the House on 7 January 1836, and was signed into law by the governor two days later. Wayne C. Temple, *Lincoln's Connections with the Illinois and Michigan Canal, His Return from Congress in '48, and His Invention* (Springfield: Illinois Bell, 1986), 6.

56. In 1834 the Illinois state legislature had eighty-one members.

57. Compare the statement of a resident of Springfield: "The most potent argument used against Vandalia, was they would feed the Illinois statesmen nothing but venison, quail, wild duck and prairie chicken. While in Springfield they would get hog meat." Caroline Oswley Brown, "Springfield Society Before the Civil War," *Journal of the Illinois State Historical Society* (April 1922), quoted in Simon, *Lincoln's Preparation for Greatness*, 81.

58. Attorney Ebenezer Peck of Chicago, a Democratic member of the Illinois state legislature, introduced the idea of a convention system during a special session in Vandalia in 1835–36. He became chief clerk of the Illinois Supreme Court (1841–45). With his son, he later established a Chicago newspaper, the *Democratic Argus*. In protest against the Kansas-Nebraska act of 1854, he broke with Douglas and became a leading Republican political strategist and organizer. Lincoln appointed him a judge of the U.S. Court of Claims.

59. Stephen Trigg Logan (1800–1880), Lincoln's second law partner, was elected judge of the First Judicial Circuit in 1835 but quit two years later because the pay was inadequate. Justin Martin Harlan (1800–1879) of Clark County was born in Ohio, where he studied law with Judge John McLean. He served on the 4th District Circuit Court many years, stepping down only in 1861. The following year Lincoln named him a U.S. Indian agent. A Princeton alumnus, Democrat John Pearson (1802–75) of Danville was a judge of the Seventh Judicial Circuit (1837–40) and a state senator (1840–43).

60. On 10 February 1835, the legislature, by a margin of four votes, chose Douglas to replace John J. Hardin as state's attorney.

61. John Wyatt, who represented Morgan County in the Illinois legislature (1832–38), was angry at Hardin because Hardin had reneged on his promise to support Wyatt's bid for a seat in the legislature in 1834. Stephen A. Douglas, "Autobiographical Sketch, September 1, 1838," in Robert W. Johannsen, ed., *The Letters of Stephen A. Douglas* (Urbana: University of Illinois Press, 1961), 63–64. Wyatt introduced a bill, written by Douglas, which authorized the legislature rather than the

governor to appoint the state's attorney. It passed and Douglas became the state's attorney. Simon, *Lincoln's Preparation for Greatness*, 107.

62. Joel A. Matteson (1808–73), governor of Illinois from 1853 to 1857, had a mansion built in 1856–57 that occupied almost an entire city block. It burned to the ground in 1873.

63. Stuart means Zachary Taylor, who was elected president in 1848 with Millard Fillmore as his running mate. Fillmore became president when Taylor died in 1850.

64. A native of New Hampshire and a Williams College alumnus, Justin Butterfield (1790–1855) practiced law in New York before moving to Chicago, where he became a prominent lawyer. From 1841 to 1844 he was U.S. district attorney in Chicago. Daniel Webster (1782–1852) was secretary of state. See Thomas F. Schwartz, " 'An Egregious Political Blunder': Justin Butterfield, Lincoln, and Illinois Whiggery," *Journal of the Abraham Lincoln Association* 8 (1986), 9–19.

65. Joshua Speed (1814–82) of Kentucky, Lincoln's closest friend, was his bunkmate in Springfield from 1837 to 1841.

66. Cf. Stuart's undated statement, Herndon-Weik Papers, Library of Congress; Paul M. Angle, ed., *Herndon's Life of Lincoln* (Cleveland: World, 1942), 246–47; Emilie Todd Helm in Katherine Helm, *Mary, Wife of Lincoln*, 107; Henry B. Rankin, *Personal Recollections of Abraham Lincoln* (New York: G. P. Putnam's Sons, 1916), 181–82. Lincoln may have turned down the Oregon offer because he felt embarrassed to take such a post while friends whom he had recommended for office were rejected. See Lincoln to Thomas Ewing, Tremont, Ill., 23 September 1849, in Roy P. Basler and Christian O. Basler, eds., *The Collected Works of Abraham Lincoln: Second Supplement, 1848–1865* (New Brunswick: Rutgers University Press, 1990), 5; and Anson G. Henry to Thomas Ewing, 24 September 1849, in Paul I. Miller, "Lincoln and the Governorship of Oregon," *Mississippi Valley Historical Review* 23, no. 3 (December 1936), 392.

Noah Brooks claimed that "Years afterward, when her husband had become President, she did not fail to remind him that her advice, when he was wavering, had restrained him from 'throwing himself away' on a distant territorial governorship." Brooks thought that Mary Lincoln "had had enough of frontier life." Brooks, *Lincoln and the Downfall of American Slavery* (New York: G. P. Putnam's Sons, 1894), 116. An Oregonian suggested that she "was afraid of Indians." A Mr. Kelly, in "Capital Pageant Review," 12 February 1936, paraphrased in an editorial, "Lincoln and Oregon," *Morning Oregonian*, 12 February 1936.

67. On the subject of Mary Todd Lincoln's temper, see Burlingame, *Inner Life of Lincoln*, 270–79, 319.

68. Nicolay Papers, Library of Congress. Ozias Mather Hatch (1814–93), Lincoln's neighbor in Springfield and political ally, served as Illinois secretary of state (1857–65).

69. In 1884 Hatch told John A. Logan,

I was at Antietam the day after the battle by invitation of Mr. Lincoln, through Marshall Lamon; of course we were the guests of General McClellan. Upon arriving at his headquarters we met departing from there, two ambulances of gentlemen in civil life, showing as we thought, that there had been a conference. As Mr. Lincoln could stay so short a time, preparations were made for a review of the troops which was done by the President and the General. Horses were furnished the other members of the party with an escort to go where we pleased. We took lunch at General Fitz-John Porter's headquarters.

The General (McClellan) submitted to Mr. Lincoln and myself a letter from one of General Lee's aides, transmitted through Genl. Porter's staff, suggesting that Genl. McClellan turn his army around, march upon Washington, displace Mr. Lincoln and seat Genl. Lee (himself) and take charge of the Government and thus save the south, or guarantee their Slaves property to them. I had known Genl. McClellan somewhat in Illinois when he was connected with the Central Railroad.

I think that was as gloomy a day as Mr. Lincoln ever saw. The army against him and the Press and Pulpit against him. So much did it affect him, that on our return home he called upon Genl. Meade at Frederick, he having been wounded, and tendered him the command of the army, which he declined. The next day Mr. and Mrs. Lincoln rode over to Genl. Hooker's headquarters and Mr. Lincoln tendered him the command, which he declined. Mr. Lincoln invited me to ride with them, which I did. In a short time Genl. Grant turned up to the great relief of the President and the country. (Hatch to Logan, Springfield, 11 March 1884, copy, box 18, folder marked "McClellan," James G. Randall Papers, Library of Congress)

70. George B. McClellan (1826–85), who commanded the Army of the Potomac (1861–62), became chief engineer of the Illinois Central Railroad in 1857.

71. Nicolay Papers, Library of Congress.

72. Charles Macallister and Henry Stebbins of New York issued bonds in 1841 to guarantee a loan to be applied to the Illinois state debt. When Illinois's finances collapsed in 1842, the bonds' value plummeted. Seventeen years later William H. Bissell (1811–60), governor of Illinois (1857–60), misunderstanding the law covering such matters, ordered a new set of bonds issued to replace the old ones.

73. Presumably Charles Macallister.

74. Nicolay Papers, Library of Congress. Clark Moulton Smith (1820–85) was Lincoln's brother-in-law. Born in Clarksville, Tennessee, he married Ann Todd in 1846. In 1852 he settled in Springfield, where he became a successful merchant and civic leader.

75. Now housed in the Lincoln Room of the University of Illinois Library.

76. Hay Papers, Brown University. On William Butler, see note 3 above.

77. The town was originally known as Calhoun. Angle, *"Here I Have Lived,"* 12–13.

78. Lincoln's family moved from Indiana to Illinois in 1830; Lincoln set out on his own in 1831 and settled in New Salem.

79. Island Grove was a settlement midway between Springfield and Jacksonville.

80. The owner of the store was James D. Henry. Lincoln, his step-brother, John D. Johnston (1811–54), and his cousin, John Hanks (1802–89), were the three boatbuilders. The person referred to as Cabanas may have been John M. Cabaniss, who was elected constable of Springfield in 1844, or his brother George.

81. When Offut's boat became stranded on a dam at New Salem, Lincoln bored a hole in the vessel to allow the water in the craft to escape.

82. Bennett Abell owned many books that Lincoln evidently borrowed.

83. Mrs. Able was born Elizabeth Owens in Green County, Kentucky, where her father, Nathaniel Owens, was a leading citizen.

84. Born in North Carolina and raised in Tennessee, Bowling Green (1787–1841) was a mentor to Lincoln. A justice of the peace in New Salem from 1831 to 1837, he headed the Democratic party in the village and was named to the Illinois Canal Commission by Governor John Reynolds in 1830. He was doorkeeper of the Illinois House of Representatives (1826–28, 1830–32) and won election as sheriff of Washington County in 1820.

85. Lincoln actually settled in New Salem in 1831 and moved to Springfield in 1837, well after the close of the Black Hawk War in 1832.

86. William Miller, the proprietor of a Springfield tavern, commanded a company in the spy battalion of the 2nd Regiment in 1831; in 1832 he was a major in the 4th Regiment, 3rd Brigade.

87. Lincoln ran for the legislature in 1832, just after returning from the Black Hawk War.

88. Brown served as a captain of the 4th Regiment of J. D. Henry's 3rd Brigade in the Black Hawk War.

89. William C. Kinney (1781–1843), a leader of Illinois's proslavery forces and lieutenant governor (1826–30), ran successfully for governor in 1830 and 1834. Thomas Ford described him as "one of the old sort of Baptist preachers; his morality was not of that pinched up kind which prevented him from using all the common arts of a candidate for office. It was said that he went forth electioneering with a Bible in one pocket and a bottle of whiskey in the other; and thus armed with 'the sword of the Lord and the spirit,' he could preach to one set of men and drink with another, and thus make himself agreeable to all." Quaife, *Ford's History of Illinois*, 1:145.

90. Nicolay and Hay paraphrase this passage as follows: "Mr. William Butler tells us that on one occasion, when Lincoln was a farm-hand at Island Grove, the famous circuit-rider, Peter Cartwright, came by, electioneering for the Legislature,

and Lincoln at once engaged in a discussion with him in the cornfield, in which the great Methodist was equally astonished at the close reasoning and the uncouth figure of Mr. Brown's extraordinary hired man." *Lincoln*, 1:101–2.

91. Peter Van Bergen (1800–1879) was a noted horseman, landowner, and moneylender in Springfield. See his interview with Nicolay elsewhere in this volume. When the store Lincoln ran with William F. Berry (1811–35) "winked out," Lincoln owed Van Bergen $154. He also owed $57.86 to William Watkins for a horse, saddle, and bridle. At the auction where the horse and compass were sold, James ("Uncle Jimmy") Short, a farmer who had settled in Sand Ridge in 1824, bought them and returned them to Lincoln.

92. Joseph Duncan (1794–1844) was governor of Illinois, 1834–38.

93. Attorney Usher Ferguson Linder (1809–76) of Coles County, an off-again-on-again Whig who became a Democrat in 1842, was known for his oratorical prowess and his drunkenness. He and Lincoln practiced law together on occasion and were friends. Charles H. Coleman, *Abraham Lincoln and Coles County, Illinois* (New Brunswick, N.J.: Scarecrow Press, 1955), 112–24.

94. Milton Hay (1817–93), uncle of Lincoln's White House secretary John Hay, was a prominent Springfield lawyer.

95. Just as his father had done, Noah W. Matheny (1815–77) served as clerk of the Sangamon County Court (1839–73). The defendants were William Tilford, William Smith, Jonathan Morgan, William H. Whittington, and Thomas Smith. A copy of the full deed is on file at the Lincoln Legal Papers, Illinois State Historical Library, Springfield. (I am grateful to William Beard and John Lupton, who located this document for me.)

96. Hay Papers, Brown University.

97. Lincoln lost his first bid for a seat in the legislature in 1832, but then won in 1834, 1836, 1838, 1840, and 1854. He declined his seat in 1854 in order to run for the U.S. Senate.

98. Henry E. Dummer (1808–78), an alumnus of Bowdoin College and Harvard Law School, was John Todd Stuart's law partner from 1833 until he moved to Beardstown in 1837.

99. Nicolay and Hay give a brief summary of this story: "when Mr. Van Bergen, who had purchased the Radford note, sued and got judgment on it, his horse and his surveying instruments were taken to pay the debt, and only by the generous intervention of a friend was he able to redeem these valuable means of living." *Lincoln*, 1:117.

100. Lincoln took his meals with Butler but lived with Joshua Speed in a room above Speed's store from 1837 to 1841.

101. Early in 1864 Lincoln drafted an order authorizing Butler and Samuel L. Casey to take control of some cotton in Louisiana and transport it to market. "Draft of Order Concerning Samuel L. Casey," 29 February 1864, in Basler et al., *Collected Works of Lincoln*, 7:213–14.

102. Hay Papers, Brown University.

103. Nicolay and Hay give a brief version of this story, which makes little use of Butler's testimony. *Lincoln*, 1:203–12.

104. James Shields (1806–79) was a leading Democrat in Illinois. He was described by an Illinois contemporary as "impulsive . . . exceedingly vain and very ambitious, and, like most ambitious men, on occasions, quite egotistical." Gustave Koerner, quoted in Simon, *Lincoln's Preparation for Greatness*, 295.

105. Julia E. Jayne (1830–77) married Lyman Trumbull in 1843; Mary Todd was her attendant at the wedding.

106. A series of pseudonymous letters appeared in the *Sangamo Journal* (Springfield) in 1842, including one by Lincoln (dated 27 August). Simeon Francis (1796–1872) was the editor.

107. John Davis Whiteside (b. 1795) of Monroe County, elected to the Illinois House of Representatives as a Democrat in 1830, 1832, 1834, and 1844, and to the state senate in 1836 from Madison County, served as state treasurer, 1837–41. His family was celebrated for its Indian fighters.

108. Dr. Revill (also spelled *Revelle* or *Revel*) W. English of Greene County won election to the Illinois House of Representatives as a Democrat in 1836, 1838, and 1840, and to the state senate in 1842 and 1844.

109. Hay Papers, Brown University. Cf. Milton Hay to John Hay, Springfield, 8 February 1887, Hay Papers, Brown University.

110. Henry B. Truett, Register of the U.S. Land Office in Galena, whom Lincoln defended in a murder trial in 1838, was the son-in-law of Congressman William L. May. Truett became mayor of Galena in 1848.

111. Dr. Samuel Houston Melvin (1829–98) owned a drug store on the northwest corner of Springfield's public square.

112. Attorney Archibald Williams (1801–63) was a Whig member of the state legislature (1832–40) and a U.S. district attorney (1849–53).

113. The legislative session was 1839–40. Ward Hill Lamon's *Life of Abraham Lincoln* (Boston: Osgood, 1872) was based in large part on interviews conducted by William H. Herndon, Lincoln's third law partner.

114. Democrat Josiah Lamborn was a lawyer from Jacksonville who eventually became attorney general of Illinois (1840–43). He ran unsuccessfully for the Illinois House of Representatives in 1834 and for the state senate in 1838. He was unflatteringly described by an Illinois lawyer and politician as a man "wholly destitute of principle," who "shamelessly took bribes from criminals prosecuted under his administration. I know myself of his having dismissed forty or fifty indictments at the Shelbyville Court, and openly displayed the money he had received from . . . them—the fruits of his maladministration. . . . He grew worse and worse towards the latter end of his life, and finally threw himself entirely away, consorting with gamblers and wasting his substance upon them. He gave himself up to intemperance, to the neglect of wife and child, whom he abandoned, and finally died miser-

ably. . . . " Usher F. Linder, *Reminiscences of the Early Bench and Bar of Illinois* (Chicago: Chicago Legal News Company, 1879), 259.

As surveyor of Sangamon County in the 1830s, John Calhoun (1806–59) of Springfield had employed Lincoln as an assistant. He was a prominent Democrat in the Illinois legislature in the late 1830s and early 1840s. He became surveyor general of Kansas in 1854 and presided over the Lecompton Constitutional Convention in 1857.

115. Another witness described the scene, which he dated "in the winter of 1839–40," thus:

A public meeting was announced to be held in the court room, "at early candle-light." It was understood that the eloquent Baker intended to expose the corruptions of the democratic administration of Martin Van Buren and that Mr. Douglas (Register of the Land Office), would reply to Baker. The announcement of the meeting, with the certainty of one and probability of both these ardent young politicians, representing the two great parties . . . always filled the largest room in Springfield, at that day, to overflowing. There were but few seats, and the standing room was fully occupied. Douglas, Baker, and a few others occupied the small platform, over which was an open hatchway to the second story, around which were a few private listeners.

Young Baker was introduced and commenced his harangue against the corruption of the democratic party. In the course of his remarks he said: "Wherever there is a land office in Illinois, there is a democratic paper; in Galena there is a land office, and a democratic paper; in Quincy there is a land office and a democratic paper; in Vandalia there is a land office and a democratic paper," and naming other important points for a land office and party papers; but when he said "in Springfield there is [a] land office and a democratic paper, and that these land offices kept these democratic papers alive with the money the people paid, when they entered government lands," insinuating corruptly, and not for a legalized compensation for advertisements and large quantities of land office blanks. At this point one of the editors of the Register pronounced the statement to be false so far as the land office and democratic paper of Springfield was concerned and stepped towards Baker, when some one cried out, "pull him down." For a moment a general if not bloody row was threatened. Directly a long pair of legs was seen issuing through the hatchway in the ceiling, and soon the person of "old Abe," as Lincoln was then called, was hanging from the hatchway, ere he made a spring beside of Baker, and from [his] manner intimated a willingness to "pitch in." Baker's good sense prompted him to say: "I may have been misinformed, and if I find I have misstated anything I will retract it publicly as I have made it." ("Reminiscences of an Old Settler of Springfield, Part Nine," unidentified clipping, ca. 1882, Brown University)

116. Hay Papers, Brown University. Jesse K. Dubois (1811–76), a friend, neighbor, and close political ally of Lincoln, was elected state auditor of Illinois in 1856.

117. In 1830.

118. Edwin Bathurst Webb (1802–58) of White County, a native of Kentucky, was a good friend of Lincoln's. He had courted Mary Todd.

119. Cf. Nicolay and Hay, *Lincoln*, 1:138.

120. The *Register* was Springfield's Democratic newspaper.

121. Robert L. Wilson (1805–80) of Athens, near New Salem, was elected a Whig state representative in 1836 and became part of the "Long Nine," which included Lincoln.

122. Eli C. Blankenship was a Springfield merchant. Taylor, a land speculator, bought property in Springfield, where he became the sheriff (1821–28). He was receiver of the general land office and promoted the town of Petersburg, near New Salem. In 1834 Blankenship, Taylor, and Duncan bought land at the geographical center of the state, laid out a town (which they named "Illiopolis"), and hoped that it would become the state capital.

123. A decade earlier Dubois had offered a less flattering assessment:

Lincoln is a singular man and I must confess I never knew him—he has for 30 years past just used me as a plaything to accomplish his own ends— but the moment he was elevated to his proud position he seemed all at once to have entirely changed his whole nature and became altogether a new being—knows no one and the road to favor is always open to his enemies whilst the door is systematically sealed to his old friends. I was not as much disappointed as my friends were at my late defeat as I never did believe Lincoln would appoint me though he time and again urged I had more talent than any of them. But I was his old friend and I could afford to be disappointed. (Dubois to Henry C. Whitney, Springfield, 6 April 1865, copy, Albert J. Beveridge Papers, Library of Congress)

While pondering his choice for an important government post, Lincoln reportedly told Dubois, "Uncle Jesse, there is no reason why I don't want to appoint you, but there is one why I can't—you are from the town I live in myself." Dubois allegedly replied: "Well, Abe, it's all right. If I were President, I don't think I'd give it to *you*, or to any other man from Illinois." New York *Tribune*, 4 May 1865. Dubois complained bitterly about the way Lincoln ignored his appeals on behalf of friends. Dubois to Lincoln, Springfield, 27 March and 6 April 1861, Lincoln Papers, Library of Congress. Cf. Dubois's undated interview with Jesse W. Weik, Weik Papers, Illinois State Historical Library, Springfield.

124. Nicolay Papers, Library of Congress. Henry S. Greene (1833–99) was admitted to the bar in 1860 after passing an examination conducted by Lincoln and others. He served in the Illinois General Assembly (1867–69) and became a law partner of Lincoln's friend Milton Hay.

125. This event occurred on 27 July 1858.

126. In his "House Divided" speech of 16 June 1858, Lincoln charged that Douglas had conspired with Presidents Franklin Pierce and James Buchanan, as well as Supreme Court Chief Justice Roger B. Taney, to throw open western territories to the spread of slavery.

127. Hay Papers, Brown University.

128. Hay Papers, Library of Congress. Stephen T. Logan (1800–1880) was Lincoln's second law partner (1841–44). Most of this interview was published in the *Abraham Lincoln Centennial Association Bulletin*, no. 12 (1 September 1928), 1–3, 5. The three sentences about Baker's handling of money were deleted. The manuscript of the interview was owned by Mrs. Alice H. Wadsworth of Mt. Morris, New York. The editorial headnote states that the "original document is dated Springfield, July 6, 1875, and is in the handwriting of William H. Herndon," suggesting that the interview was conducted by Herndon. But in fact Nicolay was the interviewer, for the original is in his handwriting.

129. The *Talisman* was a small steamboat that managed to navigate the Sangamon River to Springfield in 1832.

130. Missouri Senator Thomas Hart Benton (1816–79).

131. Lincoln denied that he had worked for William Kirkpatrick. William Dean Howells, *Life of Abraham Lincoln* (reprint, with Lincoln's emendations reproduced; Springfield: Abraham Lincoln Association, 1938), 38.

132. Jesse B. Thomas Jr. (1806–50), sat on the Illinois Supreme Court and was a target of Lincoln's withering scorn in 1840. Burlingame, *Inner World of Lincoln*, 152.

133. A newspaper in 1839 stated that "Mr. Lincoln admitted that Sangamon county had received great and important benefits, at the last session of the Legislature, in return for giving support, thro' her delegation to the system of Internal Improvements; and that though not legally bound, she is morally bound, to adhere to that system, through all time to come!" *Vandalia Free Press*, 21 February 1839, quoted in Simon, *Lincoln's Preparation for Greatness*, 99n. Simon denies that any such bargain took place; see pp. 76–105. Rodney O. Davis, an authority on the Illinois state legislature in the antebellum period, is not entirely persuaded by Simon's argument. Davis, " 'I Shall Consider the Whole People of Sangamon My Constituents': Lincoln and the Illinois General Assembly," in George L. Painter and Norbut Suits, eds., *Abraham Lincoln and the Political Process* (Springfield: Lincoln Home National Historic Site, 1994), 13–23.

134. The partnership lasted from 1841 to 1844.

135. William Henry Harrison (1773–1841) was the successful Whig candidate for the presidency in 1840.

136. Jacob M. Early had been murdered on 7 March 1838.

137. Daniel Woodson was Douglas's partner.

138. Nicolay Papers, Library of Congress. John W. Bunn (1831–1920), a leading businessman of Springfield, became president of the Marine Bank. According to J. McCan Davis, Bunn "knows many things about Lincoln. . . . He was a young man at the time of Lincoln's election as president and had not attained a place of prominence in politics. He was, however, quite familiar with much of what happened on the 'inside' here in Springfield at that time. . . . Mr. Bunn is well known to be averse to publicity and for that reason interviewers have been able to get very little from him." Davis to Ida Tarbell, Springfield, Ill., 16 May 1906, Tarbell Papers, Allegheny College.

139. In 1855 the Connecticut-born Lyman Trumbull (1813–96) beat Lincoln for a seat in the U.S. Senate, where he served until 1873.

140. Roswell Eaton Goodell (1825–1903), a Democratic politician from Ottawa, had married Governor Matteson's daughter in 1853.

2. THE WASHINGTON INTERVIEWS

1. Nicolay Papers, Library of Congress. James Kennedy Moorhead (1806–84) was a U.S. representative from Pennsylvania (1859–69). Nicolay was fortunate to obtain this interview, for nine years earlier Moorhead had refused to reveal his conversation with Lincoln to another biographer. Moorhead to Ward Hill Lamon, Pittsburgh, 12 June 1871, Jeremiah S. Black Papers, Library of Congress.

2. Alexander Cummings of Philadelphia, a political lieutenant of Cameron's, during the Civil War engaged in questionable practices while purchasing arms for the government.

3. David Davis (1815–86) of Bloomington, Illinois, a close friend and political ally of Lincoln, who named him to the U.S. Supreme Court in 1862.

4. Nicolay Papers, Library of Congress. Simon Cameron (1799–1889) was a leading Pennsylvania politician who served as Lincoln's secretary of war (1861–62).

5. A close friend and political ally of Lincoln, Leonard Swett (1825–89) was born in Maine and settled in Bloomington, Illinois, where in 1849 he met Lincoln. At the Chicago Convention, Swett played a key role, along with David Davis, in winning the nomination for Lincoln. In the transition period of 1860–61, Swett helped act as Lincoln's eyes and ears in Washington.

6. On 30 December 1860.

7. Lincoln to Cameron, Springfield, 31 December 1860, in Basler et al., *Collected Works of Lincoln*, 4:168.

8. On 3 January 1861, Lincoln told Cameron he could not offer him a cabinet portfolio after all. He made no mention of some other post. Basler et al., *Collected Works of Lincoln*, 4:169–70.

9. Vice President Hannibal Hamlin (1809–91) of Maine; Navy Secretary Gideon Welles (1802–78) of Connecticut.

10. Treasury Secretary Salmon P. Chase (1808–73) of Ohio.

11. General John A. Dix (1798–1879), commander of Union forces in New York; Edwin D. Morgan (1811–83), Republican governor of New York.

12. An allusion to George D. Morgan, a cousin and business partner to whom Governor Morgan delegated his authority (shared equally with Cummings) to purchase military supplies.

13. John Charles Fremont (1813–90) had botched his assignment as military commander of Missouri.

14. Montgomery Blair (1813–83), a Maryland politician and scion of a powerful political family, was postmaster general from 1861 to 1864. In early September, Lincoln dispatched him to St. Louis to investigate conditions. On his return, Blair recommended Fremont's removal.

15. In 1862 Lincoln named Cameron to serve as U.S. minister to Russia.

16. Ohio Senator Benjamin Franklin Wade (1800–1878), a leading Radical, was born in Massachusetts and settled in the Western Reserve section of Ohio. A militant opponent of slavery, his frank manner and hot temper won him the sobriquet "Bluff Ben." During the war he was a fierce opponent of the Confederacy and conservative Union generals. New Hampshire-born Zachariah Chandler (1813–79) at the age of twenty settled in Detroit, where he grew rich in business. Elected to the U.S. Senate in 1857, he became a truculent critic of the Confederates and their Northern sympathizers.

17. Attorney Norman B. Judd (1815–78) of Chicago was a powerful Illinois politician who chaired the Republican state central committee and served on the Republican National Committee (1856–61).

18. Judge Joseph Casey (1814–79) of Harrisburg had been Cameron's main representative at the Chicago Convention in 1860, where he demanded of Davis and Swett that Cameron be promised the treasury portfolio in Lincoln's cabinet and complete control over patronage in Pennsylvania. In response, Lincoln's managers promised that Pennsylvania would be given a cabinet seat and that they would recommend Cameron for that position. John P. Sanderson (1818–64) of Philadelphia, a leader of the Pennsylvania Republican party and a close ally of Cameron's, was an attorney, an editor, and an author. He became chief clerk of the War Department in 1861.

19. On 13 November, after John Cochrane had told his regiment (the U.S. Chasseurs in Joseph Hooker's division) that he favored emancipation of the slaves as a military measure, Cameron reportedly said: "I approve every sentiment uttered by your noble commander. All the doctrines he has laid down I approve of, as if they were uttered in my own words. These are my sentiments and the sentiments which will eventually lead to victory. 'Tis no time to talk to these people, but meet them on their own terms and treat them as enemies, and punish them as our enemies, until they learn to behave themselves. Every means which God has placed in our hands we must use, until they are subdued." Washington correspondence, 13 November 1861, *Chicago Tribune*, 14 November 1861. In December 1861, Cameron in-

cluded in his annual report the controversial recommendation that slaves be freed and armed. Lincoln ordered him to modify it.

Michael Corcoran (1827–63) was a colonel in the New York State Militia.

20. In 1847 Edwin D. and Henry A. Willard took over Fuller's City Hotel, which stood two blocks from the White House at 14th Street and Pennsylvania Avenue, remodeled it, and named it the Willard Hotel. Nathaniel Hawthorne said that "it may much more justly be called the center of Washington and the Union than . . . the Capitol, the White House, or the State Department." Pennsylvanian John W. Forney (1817–81) was editor of the *Philadelphia Press* and the *Washington Chronicle.*

21. Union recruits for service in Kentucky at first trained at Camp Joe Holt in Indiana. After the August 1861 elections in Kentucky, they set up Camp Dick Robinson in Gerard County, Kentucky.

22. Enlistments were temporarily suspended in the spring of 1862.

23. Cf. H. Nicolay, *Personal Traits of Lincoln*, 243–44.

24. Nicolay Papers, Library of Congress. Norman B. Judd (1815–78) of Chicago was a leading political ally of Lincoln who helped him win the 1860 Republican presidential nomination. The last paragraph of this interview in included in H. Nicolay, *Personal Traits of Lincoln*, 119–20.

25. Cf. H. Nicolay, *Personal Traits of Lincoln*, 123–24.

26. John M. Palmer (1817–1900), Burton C. Cook (1819–94), and Judd, as anti-Nebraska Democrats in the Illinois Senate in 1855, had voted against Lincoln and for Trumbull for a seat in the U.S. Senate.

27. Henry Winter Davis (1817–65), a cousin of David Davis, represented a Maryland district in the U.S. House of Representatives (1855–61, 1863–65).

28. Francis P. Blair Sr. (1791–1876) had been a prominent member of President Andrew Jackson's "Kitchen Cabinet."

29. Attorney Thomas A. Marshall (1817–73) of Coles County, a good friend of Lincoln's, was Speaker of the state senate. During the Civil War he was colonel of the First Illinois Cavalry.

30. Nicolay Papers, Library of Congress. Theophilus Lyle Dickey (1811–85) was a prominent attorney in Ottawa, Illinois. In 1858 he switched his allegiance from the Republican to the Democratic party.

31. The remarks about Hooker appear in H. Nicolay, *Personal Traits of Lincoln*, 256.

32. Nicolay Papers, Library of Congress. Hamilton Fish (1808–93), a prominent New York politician, was appointed by Lincoln to a board of commissioners to expedite prisoner exchanges. Later he served as President Grant's secretary of state (1869–77). This interview and the following one with Fish are unusual, for Fish put off others seeking his recollections of Lincoln. See Fish to James Redpath, Garrison (N.Y.), 1 September 1885, copy, Fish Papers, Library of Congress. At this time Nicolay asked for and received a copy of Seward's instructions to Charles Francis Adams, as amended by Lincoln, dated 21 May 1861. Fish to Nicolay, (Washington), 14 April 1874, copy, Fish Papers, Library of Congress.

33. General Ambrose E. Burnside (1824–81) led an expedition against Roanoke Island in January and February of 1862. Charles Sumner (1811–74) was a U.S. senator from Massachusetts.

34. Most of this interview appears in H. Nicolay, *Personal Traits of Lincoln*, 250–51.

35. Nicolay-Hay Papers, Illinois State Historical Library, Springfield.

36. Edward Raymond Ames (1806–79), bishop of the Methodist Episcopal Church.

37. On 26 January 1862, Ames and Fish were commissioned to provide for "the comfort and health"—but not the exchange—of Union prisoners. At Fortress Monroe they received from Confederate authorities a proposal to discuss "a General Exchange of Prisoners." Interpreting this as a rebuff of their efforts to relieve the Union captives, Fish and Ames returned to Washington. Fish and Ames to Edwin M. Stanton, Washington, 14 February 1862, Fish Papers, vol. 49, Library of Congress. S. L. M. Barlow hoped that Fish and Ames would attempt to negotiate a peace with the South. Barlow to Edwards Pierpont, New York, 28 January 1862, Stanton Papers, Library of Congress.

38. Nicolay Papers, Library of Congress. Lafayette Foster (1806–80), Republican senator from Connecticut (1855–67).

39. Cf. H. Nicolay, *Personal Traits of Lincoln*, 285.

40. Nicolay Papers, Library of Congress. Lot Myrick Morrill (1818–83), governor of Maine (1858–61), senator from Maine (1861–69), and secretary of the treasury (1876–77).

41. William Pitt Fessenden (1806–69), senator from Maine (1854–64) and secretary of the treasury (1864–65).

42. Cf. H. Nicolay, *Personal Traits of Lincoln*, 251–52.

43. Nicolay Papers, Library of Congress.

44. Nicolay Papers, Library of Congress. William Maxwell Evarts (1818–1901), prominent Republican attorney in New York.

45. Charles Francis Adams (1807–86) of Massachusetts was U.S. minister to Great Britain during the Civil War. In a eulogy delivered before the state legislature of New York on 18 April 1873, Adams claimed that Secretary of State Seward had been the guiding force behind the Lincoln administration. Adams, *An Address on the Life, Character and Services of William Henry Seward* (Albany: Weed, 1873).

46. Nicolay Papers, Library of Congress. Illinois attorney Ward Hill Lamon (1828–93) was a close friend of Lincoln, who appointed him marshal of the District of Columbia.

47. Illinois Representative Elihu B. Washburne (1816–87) was Grant's patron in Congress.

48. William Kellogg (1814–72), U.S. representative from Illinois (1857–63).

49. Cf. H. Nicolay, *Personal Traits of Lincoln*, 248–49.

50. Nicolay Papers, Library of Congress. Leonard Swett (1825–89) of Bloom-

ington, Illinois, was a close political ally of Lincoln. In 1860 he was instrumental in helping Lincoln win the presidential nomination.

51. Nicolay Papers, Library of Congress.

52. Charles A. Dana (1819–97) was managing editor of the *New York Tribune*.

53. Robert Dale Owen (1801–77), a leading emancipationist.

54. Agenor-Etienne Gasparin wrote to Lincoln on 18 July 1862. Basler et al., *Collected Works of Lincoln*, 5:356n.

55. Cf. H. Nicolay, *Personal Traits of Lincoln*, 181.

56. Nicolay Papers, Library of Congress. Morton Smith Wilkinson (1819–94) represented Minnesota in the U.S. Senate (1859–65).

57. John M. Schofield (1831–1906), commander of the Department of Missouri.

58. William T. Sherman (1820–91) got his wish: Schofield commanded a corps in Sherman's 1864 Atlanta campaign.

59. Benjamin Gratz Brown (1826–85), U.S. senator from Missouri (1863–67).

60. Nicolay Papers, Library of Congress.

61. Jacob Collamer (1791–1865), Republican senator from Vermont (1855–65).

62. Ira Harris (1802–75), Republican senator from New York (1861–67).

63. Cf. M. S. Wilkinson, "Abraham Lincoln: A Statesman's Tact," *New York Tribune*, 12 July 1885, p. 3.

64. Nicolay Papers, Library of Congress. Stephen A. Hurlbut (1815–82) was a friend of Lincoln's who served as a general in the Civil War. Born and raised in Charleston, Hurlbut had many friends in South Carolina. In Illinois he became a leading Republican.

65. James Louis Petigru (1789–1863) was a prominent South Carolina unionist.

66. General Winfield Scott (1786–1866), commander of the Union army; Robert Anderson (1805–71), commander of the Fort Sumter garrison.

67. Francis W. Pickens (1805–69), governor of South Carolina (1860–62).

68. Nicolay Papers, Library of Congress. Lyman Trumbull (1813–96), senator from Illinois (1855–73).

69. To supplement these skeletal remarks, see Trumbull's reminiscences of Lincoln in a letter to his son Walter, in Horace White, *The Life of Lyman Trumbull* (Boston and New York: Houghton, Mifflin, 1913), 426–30. Jesse W. Weik interviewed Trumbull on 8 November 1889 and recorded in his diary: "Trumbull had read our [*Weik and Herndon's*] Life of Lincoln and complimented us on it; begged to be remembered to Herndon; criticised Nicolay and Hay saying that they were more or less partisan and had fallen into old notion that Lincoln had opened way for freedom of slaves whereas Congress had really done it by two laws [*the Confiscation Acts*] passed long before the Emancipation Proclamation was issued." In commenting on these remarks, Weik later said:

I had always had an exalted opinion of Trumbull and supposed, of course, that in view of Lincoln's magnanimity and self-sacrifice in 1855 he could not only afford to be fair but even grateful; yet he seemed to be delighted that he could tell it; in other words I could not divest myself of the feeling that he was envious of Lincoln's fame and was ready, if not anxious, to discredit him as the real leader in the task of abolishing slavery. In support of his covert intimation that Lincoln had been over-praised he cited other instances which, unfortunately, or, rather, fortunately I did not record at the time. All I remember now [*is*] that the interview made a painful impression upon me and I left with a less kindly opinion of the fairness and gratitude of the man than I had before I had met him. (Weik to "Dear Mr. Pillsbury," Greencastle, Ind., 7 January 1914, security no. 0090, accession no. 91A-30, Manuscript Society Information Exchange Database, Department of Archives and Manuscripts, University Libraries, Arizona State University, Tempe)

Trumbull complained in March 1861 that he had almost no influence with the new administration: "I see little of Lincoln and know little of his policy as to appointments or anything else." Trumbull to Ozias M. Hatch, Washington, 24 March 1861, Hatch Papers, Illinois State Historical Library, Springfield.

70. Nicolay Papers, Library of Congress. John Palmer Usher (1816–89) of Indiana served as secretary of the interior (1863–65).

71. On 3 February 1865, Lincoln met secretly with three Confederate commissioners to discuss peace terms at Hampton Roads, Virginia.

72. Attorney William Tod Otto (1816–1905) of Indiana, who had been appointed assistant secretary of the interior by Usher after Caleb B. Smith retired, remained in the post until 1867. General Robert C. Schenck (1809–90) of Ohio was commander of the Middle Department.

73. One of the main prisoner-of-war camps in Richmond.

74. The Cabinet meeting was held on 5 February 1865. See Basler et al., *Collected Works of Lincoln*, 5:260–61.

75. Cf. H. Nicolay, *Personal Traits of Lincoln*, 349.

76. Nicolay Papers, Library of Congress.

77. John Edward Bouligny (1824–64) was a U.S. representative from Louisiana (1859–61) and a staunch unionist.

78. Cf. John P. Usher, *President Lincoln's Cabinet*, ed. Nelson H. Loomis (Omaha: n.p., 1925); Usher, "Abraham Lincoln: The President and His Advisers," *New York Tribune*, 13 September 1885, p. 2; Usher, "Lincoln and His Times," *Chicago Tribune*, 2 May 1882.

79. Nicolay Papers, Library of Congress. Hannibal Hamlin (1809–91) of Maine was Lincoln's vice president (1861–65).

80. Richard Mentor Johnson (1780–1850), vice president under Martin Van Buren (1837–41).

81. Nicolay Papers, Library of Congress. Joseph Holt (1807–94) was judge advocate general of the U.S. Army during the Civil War.

82. Cf. H. Nicolay, *Personal Traits of Lincoln*, 280–81.

83. John Hay noted in his diary on 18 July 1863: "Today we spent 6 hours deciding on Court Martials, the President, Judge Holt & I. I was amused at the eagerness with which the President caught at any fact which would justify him in saving the life of a condemned soldier. He was only merciless in cases where meanness or cruelty were shown." Hay Papers, Brown University.

84. Lincoln was angry at Fitz-John Porter, who was dismissed from the army for his role at Second Bull Run. Robert Todd Lincoln recalled seeing his father plainly distressed "when he learned of General Fitz-John Porter's conduct." To Orville H. Browning, the President stated "that he knew no reason to suspect any one [*involved in the Second Battle of Bull Run*] of bad faith except Fitz John Porter, and that . . . at present he believed his disobedience of orders, and his failure to go to Popes aid in the battle . . . had occasioned our defeat, and deprived us of a victory which would have terminated the war." After signing the order dismissing the general, Lincoln declared that he should have been shot. Memorandum by Rush C. Hawkins, Hombourg-les-Bains, Prussia, 17 August 1872, Hawkins Papers, Brown University; undated memorandum by Ward Hill Lamon, copy, James G. Randall Papers, Library of Congress; Pease and Randall, *Diary of Browning*, 1:589 (entry for 29 November 1862); Robert Todd Lincoln to Isaac Markens, Manchester, Vt., 13 July 1918, Robert Todd Lincoln Papers, Chicago Historical Society.

85. General Irvin McDowell (1818–85) gave the testimony.

86. James Ewell Brown Stuart (1833–64) was Robert E. Lee's cavalry commander.

87. Nicolay Papers, Library of Congress. Cf. H. Nicolay, *Personal Traits of Lincoln*, p. 230.

88. John Slidell (1793–1871) was a prominent secessionist from Louisiana who had served in the U.S. Senate (1853–61); P. G. T. Beauregard (1818–93), a leading Confederate general, had graduated from West Point in 1838.

89. Richard Delafield (1798–1873) served as superintendent of West Point (1838–45, 1856–61).

90. Lewis Cass (1782–1866) of Michigan had been the unsuccessful Democratic candidate for president in 1848. He served as Buchanan's secretary of state (1857–60).

91. Cf. Holt's letter in the *Philadelphia Press*, 15 September 1865, responding to Montgomery Blair's charges about his conduct during the secession crisis.

92. Nicolay Papers, Library of Congress.

93. Jeremiah S. Black (1810–83) served in Buchanan's cabinet as attorney general (1857–60) and as secretary of state (1860–61).

94. Nicolay Papers, Library of Congress.

95. The *Star of the West* was a merchant ship dispatched in January 1861 to relieve the Union garrison at Fort Sumter. When fired upon by South Carolina forces, it turned away and sailed back to New York.

96. Howell Cobb (1815–68) of Georgia served as secretary of the treasury in Buchanan's cabinet.

97. Robert Toombs (1810–85) represented Georgia in the U.S. Senate (1853–61) and became secretary of state for the Confederacy.

98. Jacob Thompson (1810–85) of Mississippi served as Buchanan's secretary of the interior.

99. John B. Floyd (1806–63) of Virginia served as secretary of war in Buchanan's cabinet (1857–60). Because Floyd had apparently embezzled $870,000 worth of Indian trust bonds, Buchanan asked him to resign.

100. Nicolay Papers, Library of Congress. Richard March Hoe (1812–86) of New York City was a prominent inventor and manufacturer noted for his innovations in the design of printing presses. He had been a colonel in the National Guard.

101. Cf. H. Nicolay, *Personal Traits of Lincoln*, 301–4.

102. Nicolay Papers, Library of Congress. John Sherman (1823–1900), Republican senator from Ohio (1861–77, 1881–97) and secretary of the treasury (1877–81).

103. Thurlow Weed (1797–1882) was a New York journalist and political operator who allied himself closely with Seward.

104. Sherman's report on outrages in Kansas became a Republican campaign document in the 1856 election.

105. Francis P. Blair Jr. (1821–75) of St. Louis was a prominent unionist who helped keep Missouri in the Union.

106. Nicolay Papers, Library of Congress. James Speed (1812–87), brother of Lincoln's close friend Joshua Speed, replaced Edward Bates in 1864 as U.S. attorney general.

107. Edward McManus was a White House doorkeeper.

108. Cf. H. Nicolay, *Personal Traits of Lincoln*, 273–77. See also Speed's reminiscences concerning the Gettysburg address, *Louisville Commercial*, undated clipping in the Nicolay Papers, Library of Congress; *Oration of James Speed, upon the Inauguration of the Bust of Abraham Lincoln, at Louisville, Ky.*, February 12, 1867 (Louisville: Bradley & Gilbert, 1867); *Address of Hon. James Speed Before the Society of the Loyal Legion, at Cincinnati*, May 4, 1887 (Louisville: John P. Morton, 1888).

109. Nicolay Papers, Library of Congress. Godlove Stein Orth (1817–82) was a U.S. representative from Indiana (1863–71).

110. Nicolay Papers, Library of Congress. Edward Duffield Neill (1823–93) of Minnesota served as an assistant to Nicolay and Hay in the White House (1864–65) and later as president of Macalester College. Neill's reminiscences of his service in the White House can be found in Theodore C. Blegen, ed., *Abraham Lincoln and His Mailbag: Two Documents by Edward D. Neill, One of Lincoln's Secretaries* (St. Paul: Minnesota Historical Society, 1964).

111. Nicolay Papers, Library of Congress. Henry Wilson (1812–75), a senator from Massachusetts (1855–73), served as Ulysses S. Grant's vice president (1873–75). This interview took place six days before Wilson died of the stroke that had felled him shortly before this conversation with Nicolay. Cf. H. Nicolay, *Personal Traits of Lincoln*, p. 255.

112. Nicolay Papers, Library of Congress.

113. Nicolay-Hay Papers, Illinois State Historical Library, Springfield.

114. The day before Lincoln nominated the former treasury secretary to be chief justice, he told a caller that he feared Chase's "head was so full of Presidential maggots he would never be able to get them out" and that his overweening ambition might interfere with the execution of his judicial duties. Fragment of a letter from an unidentified Massachusetts political figure (probably John B. Alley), to Josiah G. Holland, Washington, 8 August 1865, J. G. Holland Papers, New York Public Library. See also Nicolay's interview with Lafayette Foster elsewhere in this volume and John Niven, *Salmon P. Chase: A Biography* (New York: Oxford University Press, 1995), 374–75.

3. OTHER INTERVIEWS AND TWO ESSAYS BY NICOLAY

1. Nicolay-Hay Papers, Illinois State Historical Library, Springfield. Nathaniel P. Banks (1816–94) was the Union general in charge of the ill-fated Red River campaign in Louisiana in the spring of 1864.

2. David Dixon Porter (1813–91).

3. Undated document, marked "L. Mem.," Nicolay-Hay Papers, Illinois State Historical Library, Springfield. The identity of Nicolay's informant is not clear. Perhaps he was Edwin P. Parker (1836–1920), a Congregational minister from Connecticut.

4. Nicolay-Hay Papers, Illinois State Historical Library, Springfield. Frederick William Seward (1830–1915), son of Lincoln's secretary of state, William Henry Seward, served as assistant secretary of state (1861–69).

5. Cf. H. Nicolay, *Personal Traits of Lincoln*, 241–42.

6. Dictated by Nicolay to his daughter Helen, Nicolay Papers, Library of Congress. John Woodland Crisfield (1806–97) was a U.S. representative from Maryland (1861–63).

7. Summoned by the Virginia legislature, the "Old Gentlemen's Convention" opened in Washington on 4 February 1861 in a vain attempt to compromise the differences between the North and South. After three weeks it hammered out a proposal, which Congress rejected.

8. William Cabell Rives (1793–1868), a Virginia politician who had served as U.S. minister to France (1829–32, 1849–53) and a U.S. senator (1832–34, 1836–39, 1841–45).

9. Memo dated 5 January 1885, enclosed in Robert Todd Lincoln to John G. Nicolay, Washington, 5 January 1885, Hay Papers, Library of Congress. Lincoln told Nicolay that he was enclosing two memoranda, though only one exists in the Library of Congress collection. The other was doubtless the memorandum reproduced below about the Pomeroy circular. Robert Todd Lincoln seldom shared reminiscences of his father with historians. An exception was Isaac Markens. See his many letters to Markens in the Robert Todd Lincoln Papers, Chicago Historical Society.

Regarding Lincoln's order to Meade, see Gabor S. Boritt, "'Unfinished Work':

Lincoln, Meade, and Gettysburg," in Gabor S. Boritt, ed., *Lincoln's Generals* (New York: Oxford University Press, 1994), 81–120, especially 98–101; Joseph Medill's statement to Newton Macmillan, *Portland Oregonian*, 28 April 1895; and the memorandum by Rush C. Hawkins, Hombourg-les-Bains, Prussia, 17 August 1872, Hawkins Papers, Brown University. Hawkins reports, evidently based on what he had just heard, that on the day before Lincoln received Meade's dispatch saying he would not attack Lee "the President had telegraphed to Genl. Mead to follow up and attack, and [*said*] that he (the President) would hold himself responsible for the result. The telegram, as I now understand it was, read as follows: 'To Major General Mead Commanding the Army of the Potomac. You will follow up and attack Genl. Lee as soon as possible before he can cross the river. If you fail this dispatch will clear you from all responsibility and if you succeed you may destroy it.' " A Lincoln collector in Seattle allegedly bought a copy of Lincoln's order to Meade. Roger L. Scaife to Albert J. Beveridge, Boston, 27 April 1925, enclosing an undated letter from "H. L." in Seattle to Scaife, Beveridge Papers, Library of Congress.

Robert Todd Lincoln told others about this order. See the letters of R. T. Lincoln to Isaac N. Arnold, Washington, 11 November 1883 and 27 March 1884, Abraham Lincoln Collection, Chicago Historical Society, and to Isaac Markens, Washington, 6 April 1918, Robert Todd Lincoln Papers, Chicago Historical Society. See also his letters to Helen Nicolay, Manchester, Vt., 29 May 1912, and to John G. Nicolay, Chicago, 14 June 1878, and two from John G. Nicolay to R. T. Lincoln, Burlingame, Ks., 25 June 1878, draft, and Colorado Springs, 5 September 1881, all in the Nicolay Papers, Library of Congress. For more on this subject, see Isaac N. Phillips, *Abraham Lincoln: A Short Study of a Great Man and His Work* (Bloomington, Ill.: privately printed, 1901), 45–46; George H. Thacher, "Lincoln and Meade After Gettysburg," *American Historical Review* 32 (1926–27), 282–83; F. Lauriston Bullard, "President Lincoln and General Meade after Gettysburg," *Lincoln Herald* 47, no. 1 (February 1945), 30–34, and nos. 3–4 (October–December 1945), 13–16; and the remarks of Andrew S. Draper in "A Story of Lincoln," unidentified clipping dated 18 April 1887, Lincoln Museum, Fort Wayne, Ind.

In October 1863 Lincoln sent to Meade through Halleck a telegram stating, among other things, "If Gen. Meade can now attack him [*Lee*] on a field no worse than equal for us, and will do so with all the skill and courage, which he, his officers and men possess, the honor will be his if he succeeds, and the blame may be mine if he fails." Basler et al., *Collected Works of Lincoln*, 6:518.

10. Herman Haupt (1817–1905) was chief of construction and transportation of the U.S. military railroads during the Civil War. Haupt told his wife in mid-December 1862, "Last evening I went to see the President was introduced to Mrs Lincoln the Presdt. asked me to go with him to see Genl Halleck and report the position of affairs. I was with the Prest & Genl Halleck about an hour in private conference. The President remarked that as far as his observation extended 'our friend Haupt has always come up to time in his department better than almost any one else' to which Halleck at once cordially acquiesced." Herman Haupt to his wife, (Washing-

ton), 15 December 1862, Haupt Papers, Sterling Library, Yale University. See also Haupt to his wife, Washington, 18 December 1862, in the same collection.

11. Memo dated 2 January 1885, Nicolay-Hay Papers, Illinois State Historical Library, Springfield.

12. Simon P. Hanscom edited the *Washington National Republican*. Noah Brooks wrote in the fall of 1863 that

> During the last few months the Washington *Republican* has contrived to secure for itself the reputation of being the organ of the President, and accordingly a great deal of misplaced importance is sometimes attached to some of its few editorials. The solution of the puzzle is that Hanscomb, the editor, who is a pushing and persevering man, has managed to so ingratiate himself with the President that he has almost exclusive access to the office of the Executive, and there obtains from our good-natured Chief Magistrate such scanty items of news as he is willing to give out for publication, and so the enterprising editor gets up his daily column of "official intelligence," much to the annoyance and jealousy of the New York and other Washington correspondents whose dependence is upon the current news of the day, which must be gained before a single hour has blown upon its freshness. (Washington correspondence, 14 October 1863, *Sacramento Daily Union*, 7 November 1863, p. 1).

13. The "Pomeroy circular" was a document distributed to Republican leaders in February 1864 supporting Chase's presidential candidacy.

14. Chase to Lincoln, 22 February 1864; Lincoln to Chase, 23 and 29 February 1864, in Basler et al., *Collected Works of Lincoln*, 7:200n, 200, 212–13.

15. Cf. H. Nicolay, *Personal Traits of Lincoln*, 294–95.

16. Nicolay Papers, Library of Congress.

17. Cf. H. Nicolay, *Personal Traits of Lincoln*, 115–16.

18. Nicolay-Hay Papers, Illinois State Historical Library, Springfield. William McKendree Springer (1836–1903), a Springfield attorney, served in the U.S. House of Representatives from 1875 to 1895.

19. Joseph B. Stewart, a lawyer in Washington who testified at the trial of the assassination conspirators in 1865.

20. A previously unpublished essay, Nicolay Papers, Library of Congress.

21. Here Nicolay inserted Lincoln's letters to E. B Washburne (26 May 1860), to "My dear Doctor" (4 July 1860), and to Hannibal Hamlin (18 July 1860). He later crossed these out.

22. Howells (1837–1920) became one of the nation's leading novelists and critics. His book, *The Lives and Speeches of Abraham Lincoln and Hannibal Hamlin* (1860) appeared in two editions. It is valuable to scholars today because Lincoln annotated Samuel C. Parks's copy; that copy, reprinted in 1938 with Lincoln's marginal comments, constitutes a sort of autobiography.

23. Attorney Richard Wigginton Thompson (1809–1900) was a militantly anti-Catholic politician from Indiana. Thompson and Lincoln had become friends when both served in the Thirtieth Congress (1847–49). See Thompson, *Recollections of Sixteen Presidents from Washington to Lincoln* (Indianapolis: Bowen-Merrill, 1894), and two clippings in the Lincoln scrapbooks, Judd Stewart Collection, one from the *Chicago Record*, dated Terre Haute, Ind., 3 December (no year indicated), 2:29–30, and another marked "*Detroit Free Press*, 1/9/98," 3:44–47, Huntington Library, San Marino, Calif.

24. In 1856 the American party candidate Millard Fillmore had siphoned off many votes that might have gone to the Republican nominee, John Charles Fremont.

25. Lincoln to Abraham Jonas, Springfield, 21 July 1860, Basler et al., *Collected Works of Lincoln*, 4:85–86.

26. In April 1861, Thompson complained that Lincoln was ignoring his advice about patronage. Thompson to Ward Hill Lamon, Terre Haute (Ind.), 14 (or 16) April 1861, Lamon Papers, Huntington Library, San Marino, Calif.

27. Lincoln appointed Thompson collector of internal revenue for the seventh district of Indiana, a post he held for one term.

28. Hale (1799–1891) was pastor of the church from 1839 to 1866.

29. Not every Springfield clergyman looked so favorably on Lincoln. The Rev. Mr. G. W. Pendleton, who had known Lincoln for six years at the time, told Thomas W. Wheeler of Stonington, Connecticut, that:

As to his morality, or moral character, I know nothing against it. He is probably as moral as most persons who discard religion entirely in their practice.

As to his piety, it is wholly wanting. He makes no pretensions to piety. During the time I have known him, I never heard of his entering a place where God is worshipped, and I have never yet found a person who could give me any evidence that he ever went to a meeting in the town. He often goes to the railroad shop and spends the sabbath in reading Newspapers, and telling stories to the workmen, but not to the house of God. "I speak what I know and testify what I have seen." (Pendleton to Wheeler, Springfield, 1 October 1860, Connecticut Historical Society, Hartford)

30. Hale is referring to the Republican National Convention, held in Chicago in May 1860.

31. Nicolay omitted the conclusion of this letter: "There is a very striking difference between Lincoln and Douglas. Douglas is great in tricks, Lincoln in uprightness. To call him 'honest Old Abe' is not to my taste but no words can express more correctly the common opinion of him where he is well known.

"P.S. Wish I could speak as highly of his wife, as of Lincoln. On hearing of his nomination I gave my opinion that she ought to be sent to the cooper's and well secured against bursting by iron hoops. Her course since has not changed my mind." Copy, Nicolay Papers, Library of Congress.

32. Nicolay omitted the conclusion of this letter:

It is possible, I may become a sort of Campaign Committee, in spite of myself. Only *one day* before the coming of yours, I received a letter of inquiry from Rev. James A. Smith, lately of my old native Glastonbury, now of Unionville (Farmington) Conn. inquiring after Lincoln,—whether he was, as reported and as they all supposed, a *2d or 3d rate lawyer—a man of little strength &c.*—and even suggested that he supposed he should have to vote for Lincoln or Douglas. I wrote him at once, correcting his errors and letting the light into his darkness and indignantly rebuking him for writing the names of Lincoln and Douglas in the same sentence. It is a terrible tax on my sense of propriety to be obliged in this statement to bring their names so near together—but let that go. My Brother Baldwin will not be guilty of any such impropriety,—neither will Brother Smith any more—it was only a sin of ignorance and so to be winked at.

Hale's letter continues with a reference to someone who is probably Julian M. Sturtevant, president of Illinois College:

Only a short time ago, I learn, that Brother Sturtevant received a letter from Boston inquiring "if it was true *that Lincoln was a drunkard.*" Now I can easily conceive the sort of indignant reply such a letter received from Brother S. Only a few days ago, I was visited by a wealthy man—a millionaire, from a distance and he wished to see Mr. Lincoln—He must *question the Candidate.* So I went with him and he had brought two . . . important questions, which in my presence he put to Mr. Lincoln. 1. "Do you drink?" "No," was the instant reply, he has never been in the habit of drinking and has lectured against it—once in our meeting house.—2d, "Do you use tobacco?" "No, never, in any form—chewing, smoking or snuffing"—so report him to the Rev. Trask, the General-in-Chief of the forces of anti-tobacco, and let all the world know he is *a clean man,* free from the impurity and stench of the vile weed—Along with yours came a letter from Minnesota, making inquiries about the *moral character* of Mr. Lincoln—I shall give it an early reply and so enlighten a stranger, out on the borders of civilization, in reference to the character of the man towards whom the eyes of millions are turning. Would that I could say he is *a Christian as truly* as that he is an honest and true man. (Copy, Nicolay Papers, Library of Congress)

33. John Bell (1797–1869), candidate of the Constitutional Union party, carried only Kentucky, Tennessee, and Virginia. Douglas eked out a victory in Missouri with 58,801 votes; Bell received 58,372.

34. Nicolay omitted the conclusion of this letter: "It was when it was settled that Solomon was to be King of Israel the Lord came and offered his special favor and submitted it all to his choice. So, though not in the same form God comes to Lincoln, now saying: 'Ask what I shall give thee.' And, so too, very soon he will give an answer and all the land will see it in his acts. People who pray have been praying for the election of Lincoln." Copy, Nicolay Papers, Library of Congress.

35. Corporal Henry Johnson of Fayette County, Private G. B. Fancher of Coles County, and Corporal Radford N. Wyatt of Monroe County were all members of Jacob Early's company.

36. John Minor Botts (1802–69) was a prominent Virginia unionist.

37. A friend of Mary Todd Lincoln's, from Boyle County, Kentucky, Fry had been introduced to Lincoln in 1846 by John J. Hardin. In 1860 Fry campaigned for Lincoln in Pennsylvania and New York. Basler et al., *Collected Works of Lincoln*, 4:95 n; Justin G. Turner and Linda Levitt Turner, eds., *Mary Todd Lincoln: Her Life and Letters* (New York: Knopf, 1972), 91 n.

38. In 1860 John Bell of Tennessee and Edward Everett (1794–1865) of Massachusetts ran for president and vice president, respectively, on the Constitutional Union party ticket.

39. Charles H. Fisher of Philadelphia had sent Lincoln a newspaper article by his brother, Sidney G. Fisher (1808–71). The article gave a reply that George M. Dallas (1792–1864), U.S. minister to Great Britain, might have made (but did not) to Henry Peter Brougham (1778–1868), who had criticized the United States for countenancing slavery. Lincoln's allusion to a book might refer to S. G. Fisher's newly published defense of white supremacy, *The Laws of Race as Connected with Slavery*.

40. Anson G. Henry (1804–65) was a close friend and political ally of Lincoln who had moved from Illinois to Oregon in 1852.

41. This passage appears in the Springfield correspondence, 6 November 1860, in the *New York Tribune*, 10 November 1860, and was probably written by Nicolay. See Robert S. Harper, *Lincoln and the Press* (New York: McGraw-Hill, 1951), 65–66.

42. A previously unpublished essay, Nicolay Papers, Library of Congress.

43. Lincoln's brother-in-law was Clark Moulton Smith (1820–85), a prominent merchant who had married Ann Todd.

44. Edward L. Baker (1829–79), who was married to Mary Todd Lincoln's niece, was the publisher of the *Journal* from 1855 to 1874.

45. A copy of the version printed in Springfield, with many insertions in the hand of Nicolay, is to be found in the Lincoln Papers, Houghton Library, Harvard University. It is the document Nicolay gave to the press. John Hay to Charles Eliot Norton, Washington, 25 March 1889, in the same collection.

46. The bracketed words are Nicolay's.

47. Ward Hill Lamon recalled that "I had never seen Mr. Lincoln so much annoyed, so much perplexed, and for the time so angry." Lincoln, he said, "seldom manifested a spirit of anger toward his children,—this was the nearest approach to it I had ever witnessed." His anger may be partly attributed to the tone of "bored and injured virtue" that Robert exhibited when replying to his father's anxious query about the satchel. When it was finally recovered, Lincoln returned it to his son, saying: "There, Bob, see if you can't take better care of it next time." Ward Hill Lamon, *Recollections of Abraham Lincoln, 1847–1865* (2nd ed.; ed. Dorothy Lamon Teillard; Washington: privately printed, 1911), 36 Helen Nicolay, *Lincoln's Secretary: A Biography of John G. Nicolay* (New York: Longmans, Green, 1949), 64; recollections of an unidentified friend of Robert Todd Lincoln, in Wayne Whipple, "Lincoln's Love for Billy Herndon and How It Was Requited," *Illinois State Journal* (Springfield), 11 February 1912, clipping in the Lincoln Museum, Fort Wayne, Ind.

48. David Hunter (1802–86), an 1822 graduate of West Point, became a general during the Civil War.

49. Albany correspondence, probably by John Hay, 18 February 1861, *New York World*, 21 February 1861, p. 3. A clipping of this item is pasted into Hay's scrapbook, now in the possession of Robert Hoffman of Rochester, New York. I am grateful to Mr. Hoffman for allowing me to consult the scrapbook.

50. David Davis (1815–86), a close friend of Lincoln from Bloomington, Illinois, played a key role in helping Lincoln win the presidential nomination in Chicago.

INDEX

Able, Bennett, 19
Able, Mrs. Bennett (née Elizabeth Owens), 19, 138 n. 83
abolition, in Washington, D.C., 45
Abraham Lincoln: A History (Nicolay and Hay), xiv, xvi, 124 n. 20
Academy of Music (New York), 118
Adams, Charles Francis, xiii, 146 n. 32, 147 n. 45; criticizes Lincoln, 56
Albany, New York, 118, 119
Alton, Illinois, 25
Ames, Bishop Edward R., 51, 53, 147 nn. 36, 37
Anderson, Robert, 63, 77, 148 n. 66; Lincoln inquires about loyalty of, 72; Joseph Holt comments on, 72; notifies Washington about South Carolina artillery, 74
Antietam, 16, 50
Astor House (New York), 118

Baker, Edward D., 3, 28; debates Lamborn, 29, 141 n. 115; personality of, 29; as a lawyer, 38, 133 n. 45; recklessness with money, 38
Baker, Edward L., 108, 157 n. 44
Baldwin, Theron, letters about Lincoln to, 95–99
Baltimore Convention (1860), 104
Baltimore Convention (1864), 77
Baltimore women, visit Lincoln, 55–56
bank bill (Illinois), 13
Banks, Nathaniel P., xiv, 152 n. 1
Barlow, S. L. M., 147 n. 37
Bates, Edward, 151 n. 106
Bates House (Indianapolis), 109
Beardstown, Illinois, 7, 8, 9
Beauregard, P. G. T., 150 n. 88; appointment as superintendent of West Point, 71, 76
Bell, John, in 1860 campaign, 98, 101, 157 nn. 33, 38
Benton, Thomas Hart, 143 n. 130; monetary theories of, 35

Berrie, Alderman, 115
Berry, William F., 21, 139 n. 91
Bissell, William H., 17, 137 n. 72
Black, Jeremiah, 150 n. 93; loyalty of, 73; speaks with Joseph Holt, 73; sustains Robert Anderson, 77
Black Hawk, 132 n. 39
Black Hawk War, 7, 19, 20, 22, 34, 99–100
black troops, 43
Bladensburg, Maryland, 43
Blair, Francis P., Sr., 146 n. 28; advises Lincoln concerning first inaugural, 47
Blair, Francis P., Jr., 151 n. 105; and John Sherman, 80
Blair, Montgomery, 47, 65, 78, 145 n. 14, 150 n. 91; visits Fremont, 43; on emancipation, 66–67; and John Sherman, 80; as aspirant for Supreme Court, 84–85
Blankenship, Eli C., 31, 142 n. 122
Blondin, Charles, 49
Bloomington, Illinois, 15
Booth, John Wilkes, 90
Boston, Massachusetts, delegation from visits Lincoln, 48–49
Botts, John Minor, 101, 157 n. 36
Bouligny, John E., 67, 149 n. 77
bounty system, 44
Breese, Sidney, 12, 135 n. 54
Brooks, Noah, 154 n. 12
Brougham, Henry Peter, 102, 157 n. 39
Brown, B. Gratz, 61, 148 n. 59
Brown, Reuben, 20, 138 n. 88
Browning, Orville H., xiv, 28, 150 n. 84; on Nicolay's note-taking, xiv; on Lincoln's personal life, xvi; discusses religion with Lincoln, 5; criticizes first inaugural for Lincoln, 6; describes relations with Lincoln, 126 n. 1; describes visit to White House, 129 n. 15; describes Lincoln in Illinois legislature, 129 n. 20; arranges for funeral of Willie Lincoln, 130 n. 24
Browning, Mrs. Orville H. (née Eliza Caldwell), 3; befriends Lincoln, 4; Lin-

coln writes to, 4–5; relations with Lincoln, 129 n. 20
Brown University, xiv
Buchanan, James, 73, 75, 77; and John Slidell, 71–72; appearance of, 76
Buel, Clarence Clough, xvi
Buffalo, New York, 114–17
Buffalo *Morning Express*, 114–17
Bunn, John W., xiv, 144 n. 138; relations with Lincoln, 144 n. 138
Bureau of Military Justice, 68
Burlington, Iowa, 33
Burnside, Ambrose E., 147 n. 33; expedition to North Carolina, 50
Butler, William, xiv, 27, 123 n. 12; Lincoln boards with, 1; settles in Illinois, 18; relations with Lincoln, 22–25, 127 n. 3, 139 n. 101; rejects patronage offer, 23–24; on Shields-Lincoln duel, 24–25
Butler vs. Tilford, 21–22
Butterfield, Justin, 15, 136 n. 64

Cabannis, George, 19, 138 n. 80
Cabannis, John, 19, 138 n. 80
cabinet (Buchanan's), 72–75
cabinet (Lincoln's), 51–52, 65; formation of, 42, 47, 79–80; procedures of, 42; considers Fort Sumter question, 42, 64; opposes compensated emancipation, 66; religious composition of, 82–83; crisis of 1862, 87
Cairo, Illinois, 12
Calhoun, John, 28, 141 n. 114
Cameron, Simon, xiv, 72, 77, 144 n. 4; nomination to Lincoln's cabinet, 41; visits Springfield, 42; conversations with Lincoln, 42–43; visits Fremont, 43; on Chase, 44; and appointment of Stanton to Lincoln's cabinet, 44; on emancipation and use of black troops, 145 n. 19
Camp Butler, 134 n. 49
Camp Dick Robinson, 146 n. 21
Camp Joe Holt, 146 n. 21
Canada, 13
canal bill (Illinois), 12, 135 n. 55
Cartwright, Peter, 10, 20, 134 n. 45
Casey, Joseph, 43, 145 n. 18
Casey, Samuel L., 139 n. 101
Cass, Lewis, 150 n. 90; quits Buchanan's cabinet, 72–73, 75

Cavarly, Alfred W., 10, 133 n. 45
Centralia, Illinois, 48
Century Magazine, xvii
Champaign county, Illinois, 18
Chandler, Zachariah, 43, 60, 62, 70, 145 n. 16
Charleston, South Carolina, 148 n. 64; Ward Hill Lamon's mission to, 42, 63, 64; Stephen Hurlbut's mission to, 63–64; 1860 convention in, 104
Chase, Salmon P., 56, 67, 82, 85, 145 n. 10; asks Cameron to suggest purchasing agents; 42; anxiety about national finances, 44; and appointment of Stanton to Lincoln's cabinet, 52; appointed chief justice, 53, 84–85; and John Sherman, 79; Lincoln on, 85, 152 n. 114; resigns from cabinet, 89; disgust at Lincoln's levity, 90
Chicago, 44; 1860 convention in, 43, 46, 54
cholera, in Springfield, 33
Christian county, Illinois, 10, 35
Cincinnati, Ohio, xi, 34
Clapp, A. M., 115
Clary, John, 133 n. 42
Clary's Grove boys, 9, 133 n. 42
Clay, Henry, 30
"Claybanks," 60
Clear Lake, Illinois, 11
Cleveland, Ohio, 115
Clinton, Illinois, 32
Cobb, Howell, 150 n. 96; hatred for the Union, 74
Cochrane, John, 145 n. 19
Colby, Robert, on Nicolay's personality, xiii
Collamer, Jacob, 62, 84, 148 n. 61
Columbus, Ohio, 113, 118
Committee on the Conduct of the War, 83–84
compensated emancipation, 66
Confederate States of America, 64, 119
Constitutional Union party, 157 nn. 33, 38
Cook, Burton C., 45, 146 n. 26
Coolidge, Calvin, xvii
Coombs, Leslie, letter to Lincoln, 101–2
Corcoran, Michael, 43, 145–46 n. 19
Cornell, Charles G., 119
cotton speculators, 86
court bill (Illinois), 13
courts martial, 68–71, 83

Crisfield, John W., 87, 88, 152 n. 6
Cummings, Alexander, 41, 42–43, 144 n. 2

Dallas, George M., 102, 157 n. 39
Dana, Charles A., 125 n. 29, 148 n. 52; criticizes Lincoln administration, 58
Danley, Samuel, 11, 134 n. 49
Danville, Illinois, 38
Davis, David, 32, 41, 43, 46, 47, 83, 118, 144 n. 3, 145 n. 18, 158 n. 50
Davis, Henry Winter, 47, 146 n. 27
Davis, Jefferson, 52, 119
Davis, Rodney O., 143 n. 133
Dawson, John, 8, 9, 132 n. 37
Decatur, Illinois, Republican convention at, 46
Delafield, Richard, 71, 150 n. 89
Dement, John, 8, 132 n. 39
Democratic party, 13, 46, 104
Dickey, T. Lyle, xiv, 48, 57, 146 n. 30
Dix, John A., 42, 145 n. 11
Dixon, Illinois, 7, 9, 10
Douglas, Stephen A., 3, 14, 28, 54, 98, 135 n. 58, 143 n. 126; in 1858 campaign, xii, 32, 44–45, 48; and Matilda Edwards, 1; elected state's attorney, 13, 139 nn. 60, 61; in Illinois legislature, 30; in Early case, 39; on role of clergy in politics, 95; wins Missouri (1860), 157 n. 33
draft, in North, 44
Dubois, Jesse K., xiv, 82, 142 n. 116; criticizes Lincoln, 142 n. 123
Dummer, Henry E., 22, 139 n. 98
Duncan, Joseph, 21, 31, 139 n. 92

Early, Jacob, 133 n. 40; in Black Hawk War, 8, 9, 133 nn. 41, 44; 144 n. 136; murder of, 39, 144 n. 136
Eckert, Thomas T., 125 n. 29
Edwards, Matilda, 1, 2, 128 nn. 7, 8
Edwards, Ninian W., 1, 2, 40; character of, 127 n. 4
election campaigns: of 1832, 10, 20, 35–36; of 1834, 11, 36; of 1840, 39; of 1856, xii, 103; of 1858, 32–33; of 1860, 91–106
emancipation proclamation 58, 148 n. 69
English, Revill W., 25, 140 n. 108
Episcopalians, in Lincoln's cabinet, 82–83
Evarts, William M., 147 n. 44
Everett, Edward, 101, 157 n. 38

Fancher, G. B., 100, 157 n. 35
Fessenden, William P., 62, 147 n. 41; and William H. Seward, 54
Fillmore, Millard, 15, 115, 166 n. 63
Fish, Hamilton, 53, 146 n. 32
Fisher, Charles H., 157 n. 39; Lincoln's letter to, 102–3
Floyd, John B., 151 n. 99; character of, 74–75, 76
Ford, Thomas, 10, 13, 134 n. 45; quoted, 138 n. 89
Ford's Theater, 90
Forney, John W., 43, 146 n. 20
Forquer, George, 7, 10, 132 n. 32
Fort Johnson, 132 n. 36
Fort Monroe, 53
Fort Sumter, 42, 63, 64, 77
Foster, Lafayette, xiv, 147 n. 38
Four Lakes, Wisconsin, 8, 9
Francis, Simeon, 24, 132 n. 33, 140 n. 106
Freeport, Illinois, 45
Fremont, John C., 145 n. 13; conversation with Simon Cameron, 43
Fry, John B., 157 n. 37; receives letter from Lincoln, 101–2
fugitive slave act, 45

Galena, Illinois, 8, 9, 132 n. 39, 140 n. 110
Galveston, Texas, 86
Garbutt, Zachariah N., xi
Gasparin, Agenor-Etienne, 59
General Land Office, 15
Gettysburg, 81, 82, 88, 152 n. 9
Gilder, Richard Watson, 126 n. 36
Goodell, Roswell E., 39, 144 n. 140
Grant, U. S., 137 n. 69, 146 n. 32, 151 n. 111; Lincoln's support of, 57
Gratiot's Grove, 100
Greeley, Horace, xii
Green, Bowling, 19, 138 n. 84
Green, Peter, 10, 133 n. 45
Greene, Henry S., xiv, 143 n. 124
Gurley, Phineas D., 130 n. 24

Hale, Albert, 155 n. 28; describes Lincoln, 95–99
Halleck, Henry W., 86, 153 n. 10
Hamlin, Hannibal, xiv, 42, 144 n. 9, 149 n. 79, 154 n. 21
Hampton Roads conference, 65, 66, 94

Hanks, John, 138 n. 80
Hanscom, Simon P., 89, 154 n. 12
Hardin, John J., 3, 13, 25, 28, 135 n. 60
Harlan, Justin M., 13, 135 n. 59
Harris, Ira, 62, 87, 148 n. 62
Harrisburg, Pennsylvania, 120
Harrison, George M., 9, 10, 99–100, 133 n. 44
Harrison, William Henry, 39, 143 n. 135
Harvard College, 88
Hatch, Ozias M., xi, xii, xiv, 136 n. 68; on Lincoln's visit to McClellan, 136–37 n. 69
Haupt, Herman, 88, 153 n. 10
Hawkins, Rush, 153 n. 9
Hawthorne, Nathaniel, 146 n. 20
Hay, John, xiv–xvii, 89, 150 n. 83, 158 n. 49
Hay, Milton, xiv, 139 n. 94; on Lincoln's depression, xvi; friendship with Lincoln, 21
Hayes, Rutherford, 93
Henderson's Point, Illinois, 22
Henry, Anson G., 157 n. 40; Lincoln's letter to, 104–5
Henry, James D., 9, 19, 133 n. 43, 138 n. 80
Herndon, William H., xiv, 28, 140 n. 113, 143 n. 128, 148 n. 69
Hoe, Richard M., 151 n. 100
Holt, Joseph, xiv, 149 n. 81, 150 n. 83; reviews courts martial decisions with Lincoln, 68–71; on Fitz John Porter, 70–71; and Buchanan, 71–72; on Robert Anderson, 72; consults with Lewis Cass, 72–73, 75; joins Buchanan's cabinet, 73–74; and John Slidell, 73–74, 76–77; recruits troops, 74; on Howell Cobb, 74; on Robert Toombs, 74; on Jacob Thompson, 74; on John B. Floyd, 74–75; on Buchanan's despair, 76
Hood, Thomas, 3, 129 n. 15
Hooker, Joseph, 50, 137 n. 69, 145 n. 19
Howard, James Quay, 134 n. 50
Howells, William Dean, xii, 92, 154 n. 22
Hubbard, Gurdon, 12, 134 n. 53
Hunter, David, 158 n. 48; and black troops, 43; injured protecting Lincoln, 114, 116
Hurlbut, Stephen A., xiv, 148 n. 64; visits Charleston, 63–64

Iles, Elijah, 132 n. 36; in Black Hawk War, 8, 9; as land developer, 33, 34

Illinois, migration into, from Kentucky, 34–35
Illinois and Michigan canal, 12
Illinois Central Railroad, 12, 16
Illinois River, 12
Illinois State Agricultural College, 18
Illinois State Journal, 108. *See also San-amo Journal*; Baker, Edward L.; Francis, Simeon
Illinois state legislature, 3–4, 12–13, 47
Illiopolis, Illinois, 21, 31
Independence Hall, Philadelphia, 120
Indianapolis, Indiana, 6, 108–9, 118
"internal improvement mania," in Illinois, 12
Island Grove, Illinois, 18, 20, 138 n. 79

Jackson, Andrew, 102, 133 n. 45
Jacksonville, Illinois, 28, 31
Jayne, Julia, 24, 140 n. 105
Johnson, Andrew, xiii, 56
Johnson, Henry, 100, 157 n. 35
Johnson, Richard M., 67, 149 n. 80
Johnston, John D., 19, 138 n. 80
Judd, Norman B., xiv, 48, 145 n. 17, 146 n. 24

Kellogg, William, 57, 147 n. 48
Kentucky, 19, 34, 35, 74; Lincoln's anxiety about loyalty of, 43
Kinney, William C. 20, 138 n. 89
Kirkpatrick, William, 36
Know Nothings, 93, 95
Kreismann, Herman, xii

Lamborn, Josiah, 28, 29, 140 n. 114
Lamon, Ward Hill, xiv, 16, 137 n. 69, 147 n. 46; biography of Lincoln by, 3, 18, 28; Lincoln's relations with, 42; mission to Charleston, 42, 63, 64; protects Lincoln, 113–14; on Lincoln's anger, 158 n. 47
Lamon, Mrs. Ward Hill, 3, 5
Lawrence county, Illinois, 29
Lawrenceville, Illinois, 30
lawyers, in Illinois in 1830s, 25–26, 37
Lee, Robert E., 88, 89, 137 n. 69
Leland Hotel, Springfield, 1
Library of Congress, xiv
Lick Creek, 35

Lincoln, Abraham
  ambition of, 6–7, 37, 78
  amiability of, 19, 20, 36
  on Anderson, Robert, 72
  anger of, 17, 49, 67, 78–79, 88, 158 n. 47
  appearance of, 20, 30, 35, 45
  assassination of, 90
  assassination threats, indifference to, 71
  athleticism of, 20
  awkwardness of, 20, 27, 30
  Black Hawk War service of, 7–10, 19–20, 100
  on Burnside's expedition in North Carolina, 50
  on Cameron, Simon, 41
  caution of, 94
  character of, 6, 20, 26–27, 31, 96, 156 n. 32
  on Chase, Salmon P., 53, 85, 87, 152 n. 114
  and Chicago Convention (1860), 46
  churchgoing habits of, 95–96, 155 n. 29
  conscientiousness of, 6, 83
  conversations with: Bishop Edward R. Ames, 52; O. H. Browning, 5; Mrs. O. H. Browning, 4; William Butler, 22–24; cabinet, 66, 67; callers in Springfield (1860), 96, 98–99, 156 n. 32; Simon Cameron, 42; Zachariah Chandler, 60; T. Lyle Dickey, 49–50; J. K. Dubois, 31; Hamilton Fish, 50, 52; Lafayette Foster, 53; Albert Hale, 97–98; O. M. Hatch, 16, 17; Joseph Holt, 69–72; Stephen A. Hurlbut, 62–63; Norman B. Judd, 44–48; Stephen T. Logan, 37, 38; James K. Moorhead, 41; Lot M. Morrill, 54–55; mothers of soldiers, 55–56, 80–82; E. D. Neill, 83; Ebenezer Peck, 45; C. M. Smith, 17–18; Thaddeus Stevens, 77–79; John Todd Stuart, 14; Charles Sumner, 50; Leonard Swett, 58–59; Benjamin F. Wade, 57, 84; Morton S. Wilkinson, 60, 61; Henry Wilson, 85
  correspondence of, 91
  on cotton speculators, 86–87
  courtship with Mary Todd, xvi, 1–2, 128 n. 10
  debates with: John Calhoun, 28; Peter Cartwright, 20; Stephen A. Douglas, 32–33, 44–45, 48

  debts of, 21, 22, 33, 139 n. 91
  depression of, xvi, 1–2, 3
  domestic woes of, 3
  duel with James Shields, 24–25
  egalitarianism of, 38
  and emancipation, 58–59, 66–67
  fatalism of, 7, 14
  forbearance of, 85, 95, 103–4
  gloom of, 1–3, 31, 32, 38, 61, 66, 69, 137
  on Hooker, Joseph, 50
  humor of, 4, 8, 20, 57
  Illinois, moves with family to, 29–30
  individuality of, 20, 26, 35
  integrity of, 96
  as inventor, 18
  journey to Washington (1861), 5–6, 108–20
  and Know Nothings, 93
  law office of, 27, 29
  as lawyer, 28, 37, 38–39
  leadership of, 28, 30, 31, 37, 55, 94
  as legislator, 12–13, 30, 36–37, 129–30 n. 20
  letters to: Mrs. O. H. Browning 3–5; Charles H. Fisher, 102–3; John B. Fry, 101; Anson G. Henry, 104–5; C. M. Smith, 17; persons seeking a political statement, 92; prospective biographers, 91–92
  magnetism of, 110
  mathematical skill of, 26
  on McClellan, George, 16
  on Missouri affairs, 60
  modesty of, 87, 97–98
  at New Salem, 19–21, 33, 35–36, 37–38
  on Owen, Robert Dale, 59
  pardons of, 53, 55–56, 68–71, 80–82, 150 n. 83
  patience of, 103–4
  patronage and, 82, 94, 96, 97
  personality of, 2, 103–4
  piety of, 155 n. 29
  and political campaigns: of 1832, 10, 35; of 1840, 39; of 1856, 103; of 1858, 32–33, 44–45, 103; of 1860, 91–106
  on Pomeroy circular, 89
  popularity of, 8–9, 10, 20, 26–27, 30, 35, 105–6
  on Porter, Fitz John, 150 n. 84
  profanity used by, 17, 67

as public speaker, 28, 35, 39

reading habits of, 37, 38

reception of, in 1861: in Buffalo, 114–15; in Columbus, 113–14; in Pittsburgh, 114

on his reelection chances, 58

relations with: E. D. Baker, 29, 141 n. 115; O. H. Browning, 126 n. 1; Mrs. O. H. Browning, 129–30 n. 20; John W. Bunn, 144 n. 138; William Butler, 23, 24, 127 n. 3; Salmon P. Chase, 89; T. Lyle Dickey, 48; Jesse K. Dubois, 142 n. 123; Matilda Edwards, 128 n. 8; William M. Evarts, 56; Lafayette Foster, 53; U. S. Grant, 57; Albert Hale, 97; Hannibal Hamlin, 67–68; Simon P. Hanscom, 154 n. 12; George M. Harrison, 99–100; Herman Haupt, 153 n. 10; Milton Hay, 21; Ward Hill Lamon, 42; George McClellan, 136 n. 69; John G. Nicolay, xi–xiii; Richard W. Thompson, 93–94; Benjamin F. Wade, 83–84

reliability of, 11, 28

religious views of, 5, 14–15, 87, 96, 130 n. 24

and removal of Illinois capital to Springfield, 31, 34, 36–37, 143 n. 133

on his role as president, 54–55

sarcasm of, 16, 132 n. 32

self-control of, 103–4

slavery, views on, 5, 102–3

sociability of, 103

social awkwardness of, 3–4, 27

speeches, method of composing, 107; for first inaugural, 6, 47, 107, 109–10; at Clinton, Illinois, 32–33; en route to Washington (1861), 110, 112–13; at Trenton, 120

as storyteller, 20, 27

superstitiousness of, 6

as surveyor, 26, 33

as teetotaler, 33, 38, 156 n. 32

temper of, 36

and tobacco, 156 n. 32

war, attempts to avert, 17

weeps, 88

as Whig spokesman, 36

work habits of, 83

as wrestler, 8, 19

Lincoln, Mary Todd, 50, 90; temper of, xvi, 15; courtship with Lincoln, 1–2; personality of, 1, 127 n. 6; madness of, 3; opposes Lincoln's plan to retire to Springfield, 14; opposes move to Oregon, 15, 136 n. 66; intellectual power of, 15; criticized, 15, 155 n. 31; belittles James Shields, 24; as hostess, 46; as church member, 95; pride of, 155 n. 31

Lincoln, Robert Todd, xv, 150 n. 84, 152 n. 9; relations with Nicolay, xiv, 124 n. 24; censors biography by Nicolay and Hay, xiv; sensitivity of, xvi; misplaces Lincoln's inaugural address, 108–9

Lincoln, Thomas ("Tad"), 130 n. 24

Lincoln, William W., death of, 130 n. 24

Linder, Usher, 21, 139 n. 93

Logan, David, 38

Logan, Sally. See Lamon, Mrs. Ward Hill

Logan, Stephen T., xiv, 13, 39, 135 n. 59, 143 n. 128; as a lawyer, 28; settles in Springfield, 34; meets Lincoln, 35; as a judge, 36; as Lincoln's law partner, 37; as mentor to Lincoln, 38

Logan county, Illinois, 10, 35

"Lost Townships" letters, 24

Louisiana, 67

Macallister, Charles, 16–17, 137 n. 72

Macallister and Stebbins bonds, 17

Madison, Wisconsin, 8, 9

Markens, Isaac, 152 n. 9

Marshall, Thomas A., 48, 146 n. 29

Masked Ball (Verdi), 118

Mason county, Illinois, 35

Matheny, James H., 27

Matheny, Noah, 22, 139 n. 95

Matteson, Joel, 14, 17, 39–40, 136 n. 62

May, William, 133 n. 45, 140 n. 110

McClellan, George, 16, 50, 70, 84, 136 n. 69, 137 n. 70

McClure, Alexander K., xiii

McClure's Magazine, xv

McConnel, Murray, 10, 133 n. 45

McDowell, Irvin, 70, 150 n. 85

McManus, Edward, 80, 81, 151 n. 107

Meade, George G., 88, 137 n. 69; Lincoln's anger at, 152 n. 9

Melvin, Samuel H., 27, 140 n. 111

Menard county, Illinois, 10, 11, 35

Mendota, Illinois, 45

Methodists, Lincoln's need to give patronage to, 82
Miller, William, 19, 133 n. 42, 138 n. 86
Mississippi River, 33
Missouri, xi, 59, 60, 61, 80, 98
Missouri Democrat (St. Louis), xii
Moffett, Thomas, 7
Monroe, James, 102
Montgomery, Alabama, 119, 120
Moorhead, James K., xiv, 144 n. 1
Morgan, Edwin D., 42, 145 n. 11
Morgan, George D., 43, 145 n. 12
Morrill, Lot M., xiv, 147 n. 40
Morris, Achilles, 10, 136 n. 46
Morton, Oliver P., 6

Neill, Edward D., 151 n. 110
Nevins, Allan, 124 n. 20
New Salem, Illinois, 7, 10, 11, 19, 33, 35, 37–38
New York *Tribune*, 58, 105–6
New York *World*, 117–18
Nicolay, Helen, xiv
Nicolay, John G., 89; birth of, xi; education of, xi; shyness of, xi; becomes clerk to O. M. Hatch, xii; becomes Lincoln's secretary, xii, 123 n. 12; criticized, xii,196xiii; personality of, xiii, 124 n. 16; as marshal of U.S. Supreme Court, xiii, xiv; as U.S. consul in Paris, xiii; writes biography of Lincoln, xiv; conducts interviews, xiv, xv; refuses to help Ida Tarbell, xv; skepticism about human memory, xv; relates story about S. P. Chase, 90

Offutt, Denton, 134 n. 48, 138 n. 81
Ohio River, 12
Oregon, 15, 104
Orth, Godlove, xiv, 151 n. 109
Ottawa, Illinois, 144 n. 140; and Black Hawk War, 7, 8, 9, 132 n. 35; and 1858 Lincoln-Douglas debates, 45, 48
Otto, William T., 65, 149 n. 72
Owen, Robert Dale, 58, 59, 148 n. 53
Owens, Elizabeth. *See* Able, Mrs. Bennett

Palmer, John M., 45, 146 n. 26
Parker, Dr., 152 n. 3
Parks, Samuel C., 154 n. 22
Peace Convention (1861), 47, 75, 87–88

Pearson, John, 13, 135 n. 59
Peck, Ebenezer, 13, 45, 135 n. 58
Pendleton, G. W., criticizes Lincoln, 155 n. 2
Peoria, Illinois, 10, 31
Personal Traits of Abraham Lincoln (Helen Nicolay), xiv
Peru, Illinois, 12
Petigrew, James L. *See* Pettigru, James L.
Petigru, James L., 63, 64, 148 n. 65
Philadelphia, 120
Phillips, Miss, 119
Pickens, Francis W., 63, 64, 148 n. 67
Pierce, Franklin, 143 n. 126
Pierson, John. *See* Pearson, John
Pike county, Illinois, xi
Pike County Free Press, xi
Pittsburgh, Pennsylvania, 114
Pittsfield, Illinois, xi, xiv
Point Lookout, Maryland, 55
Pomeroy circular, 89, 154 n. 13
Pope, John, 70, 71
Porter, David D., 86, 152 n. 2
Porter, Fitz John, 137 n. 69, 150 n. 84; court martial of, 70–71

Quincy, Illinois, 3, 4, 6, 28, 141 n. 115
Quinton, Richard, 12, 134 n. 51

Randall, James G., xvii
Red River expedition, 86
Republican party, 48, 61–62, 78
Reynolds, John, 138 n. 84
Richmond, Virginia, 52, 149 n. 73
Ritchie, Donald, xviii
Rives, William C., 88, 152 n. 8
Roanoke Island, North Carolina, 50
Rock Island, Illinois, 7, 9
Rock River, 9, 10, 19
Rosecrans, William S., 60
Rushville, Illinois, 7, 8, 9
Russian mission, and Simon Cameron, 43

Sanderson, John P., 43, 145 n. 18
Sangamo Journal, 7, 24, 140 n. 106. *See also Illinois State Journal*
Sangamon county, Illinois, 10, 20, 35, 103
Sangamon River, 19, 34
Sangamon Town, Illinois, 19
Schenck, Robert C., 65, 66, 149 n. 72
Schofield, John M., 59, 60, 61, 148 n. 57

Scott, Winfield, 63, 148 n. 66
Scripps, John L., xii
secessionists, 62–63, 72, 100–101
Seward, Frederick W., 152 n. 4
Seward, William H., 52, 82, 102; deals with Confederate commissioners, 42; accuses Cameron of cheating him, 43; visits Cameron, 43; presidential candidacy of, 47, 54; respect of, for Lincoln, 56; on Southern unionism, 62–63; meddlesomeness of, 65; at Hampton Roads conference, 65, 94; on emancipation proclamation, 67; denounced by Robert Schenck, 65–66; misses cabinet discussion of compensated emancipation, 66; supports John Sherman for cabinet post, 79; offered seat in Lincoln's cabinet, 94
Shastid, Thomas Wesley, xi
Sherman, John, xiv, 151 n. 102; as potential member of cabinet, 79–80; and Kansas troubles, 80
Sherman, William T., 43, 60, 61, 148 n. 58
Shields, James, 24, 39, 140 n. 104
Short, James ("Uncle Jimmy"), 139 n. 91
Shurtleff College, 18
Simon, Paul, 143 n. 133
Slidell, John, 150 n. 88; insolence of, 71, 76–77; hostility toward Joseph Holt, 73–74
Smith, Caleb B., 149 n. 72
Smith, Clark M., xiv, 107, 137 n. 74, 157 n. 43
Smith, James A., 156 n. 32
Soldiers Home, 88
Speed, Fanny, 15
Speed, James, xiv, 151 n. 106
Speed, Joshua, 15, 136 n. 65, 139 n. 100; informs Lincoln about Kentucky affairs, 43
Spring Creek, Illinois, 19, 35
Springer, William M., 154 n. 18
Springfield, Illinois, xiv, 5, 14, 18, 21, 28, 46, 91, 105–7; project to locate seat of state government at, 31, 34, 36–37, 143 n. 133
Springfield *Register*, 30, 141 n. 115, 142 n. 120
Stanton, Edwin M., 44, 51, 65, 71, 73; in Buchanan's cabinet, 76; profanity of, 82
Star of the West (ship), 74, 150 n. 95
Stebbins, Henry, 16, 137 n. 72

Stevens, Thaddeus, conversation with Lincoln, 77–79
Stewart, Joseph B., 90, 154 n. 19
Stillman, Isiah, 7, 9, 132 n. 35
St. Louis, 18
Stoddard, William O., xv, 124 n. 16, 125 n. 28; quoted, xiii
Strong, Newton D., 2, 128 n. 11
Stuart, James Ewell Brown, 71, 150 n. 86
Stuart, John Todd, xiv, 9, 27, 28, 39; in 1832 legislative campaign, 10, 35; in 1834 legislative campaign, 11–12, 134 n. 50; as caucus leader, 21; advises Lincoln to study law, 22; as legislative leader, 30; nicknames of, 30; as a lawyer, 37
Sturdevant, Julian M., 156 n. 32
Sumner, Charles, xiii, 84, 147 n. 33; conversation with Lincoln about Burnside's expedition, 50–51; Hamilton Fish on, 51
Swett, Leonard, xiv, 42, 43, 47, 144 n. 5, 145 n. 18, 147 n. 50

Talisman, 34, 143 n. 129
Taney, Roger B., 143 n. 126
Tarbell, Ida M., xv
Taylor, Edmund Dick, 10, 134 n. 46
Taylor, John, 31, 142 n. 122
Tazewell county, Illinois, 24
Terre Haute, Indiana, 93
Thayer, William Makepeace, 4
Thomas, Jesse, 36, 143 n. 132
Thompson, Jacob, 151 n. 98; character of, 74
Thompson, Richard W., 93, 94, 155 nn. 23, 27
Tilford, William, 21
Toombs, Robert, 151 n. 97; hatred for Union, 74
Tremont, Illinois, 15, 25
Trenton, New Jersey, 120
Truett, Henry B., 140 n. 110; defended by Lincoln, 27, 39, 140 n. 110
Trumbull, Lyman, xiv, 140 n. 105, 144 n. 139, 148 n. 68; elected to U.S. Senate, 39–40, 45; jealousy of Lincoln, 148 n. 69
Trumbull, Mrs. Lyman. *See* Jayne, Julia

Usher, John P. xiv, 149 n. 70

Van Bergen, Peter, xiv, 21, 22, 23, 139 nn. 91, 99
Van Buren, Martin, 67, 141 n. 115
Vandalia, Illinois, 3, 12, 13, 21, 22, 29, 31, 34, 37, 135 n. 57, 141 n. 115
vice presidency, Hannibal Hamlin on, 67
Vicksburg, 57

Wabash River, 39
Wade, Benjamin F., 43, 57, 61, 62, 83–84, 145 n. 16
Wadsworth House, 116
Washburne, Elihu B., 57, 147 n. 47, 154 n. 21
Washington monument, 18
Watkins, William, 139 n. 91
Webb, Edwin B., 30, 31, 142 n. 118
Webster, Daniel, 15, 136 n. 64
Weed, Thurlow, 17, 151 n. 103; favors John Sherman for cabinet post, 79
Weidrich, Major, 115

Weik, Jesse W., 148–49 n. 69
Welles, Gideon, 42, 144 n. 9
West Point, 76
Whig party, 31, 93
Whiteside, John David, 24, 140 n. 107
Wide Awakes, 111
Wilkinson, Morton S., xiv, 148 n. 56
Willard, Edwin D., 146 n. 20
Willard, Henry A., 146 n. 20
Willards Hotel, 43
Williams, Archibald, 28, 140 n. 112
Wilson, Douglas L., xvi–xviii
Wilson, Henry, xiv, 151 n. 111
Wilson, Robert L., 31, 142 n. 121
Woodson, Daniel, 39, 144 n. 137
Wyatt, John, 13–14, 135 n. 61
Wyatt, Radford N., 100, 157 n. 35

Young, John Russell, xiii

Michael Burlingame, author of *The Inner World of Abraham Lincoln,* is a professor of history at Connecticut College in New London. He is currently editing a new version of the Civil War diary of John Hay and an edition of Hay's letters and journalism (1860–65).